M000211646

"Raw. Authentic. Poignant. The reader is immediately drawn into this memoir of the beloved son Judi and Brian suddenly lost that is written as only a mother who has experienced the tragic loss of a child could write. As you read about Jenson's life and as you laugh and cry and mourn with Judi, you will come to know him personally and appreciate the gift he was to his family. You will also observe the overwhelming and immense emotions a mother experiences as she learns to navigate a new life without her son."

—Karen L. Doherty, mom of Lauren,
who took her life on 8/4/2010

"Judi has done a masterful job in writing of the life and suicidal death of her precious son Jenson. Her very frank, detailed, and unvarnished account opens a window on her deep loss, grieving, and continuing love for her Jenson. She teaches us how to minister to those who experience such a deep loss with careful love and understanding. I could not put this book down. It has changed how I will minister to those in great loss. Throughout this account, Judi's deep, abiding faith and hope in Christ shine through. Thank you, Judi, for this book."

—Perry Jones, executive director,
Capital City Rescue Mission

"Superbly crafted, and overflowing with exceptional tenacity, tenderness, and an honesty that is beautiful to witness, *Empty Shoes by the Door* is an essential handbook—a modern-day *Pilgrim's Progress*. It is both a powerful affirmation, and a sincere call to arms for anyone called to withstand the waves, endure the flames, and simply keep walking, through the darkest times life can hurl our way. It is a stunning example of how to go on, without those we love the most. It is also a magnificent testimony to the indestructible power of maternal love which, even in the agony of deepest loss, remains constant, uncompromised, and unbroken."

—Maria Riccio Bryce, composer of "Hearts of Fire," lyricist, pianist, director

"Although focused on the suicidal death of her beloved son, this book is of great value for all who strive to show compassion in a sensitive manner and those who are called upon to comfort grieving hearts. No two recipients of compassion and comfort are identical, and we should strive, guided by the Spirit, to recognize the uniqueness of each situation. As we err on the side of sensitivity, we will minister more effectively for the long term. I appreciate Judi's courage and honesty as she shares Jenson's, Brian's, and her story."

—David Treadwell, executive director emeritus, Central Union Mission, Washington, DC

"Judi Merriam's book . . . is personal, powerful, painful, yet at times surprisingly practical. It will take you into a 'valley' where few willingly want to go. Today, editorial writers proclaim suicide to be a growing national tragedy, even as clergy understand it as a tightly-held family secret. Do those left behind ever get over it? No. But many get through it with the help of families, friends, faith and gut-wrenchingly honest companions like Judi."

—William A Ritter, United Methodist pastor, former visiting professor of preaching, Duke Divinity School, author of *Take the Dimness of My Soul Away: Healing After a Loved One's Suicide* and *Nudging the Heart: I Meant What I Said from the Pulpit*

"In *Empty Shoes by the Door* Judi Merriam courageously shares the tragic story of her precious son's completely unexpected suicide and the sometimes-helpful but often worse-than-unhelpful ways people with the best of intentions responded to Judi's grieving family . . . *Empty Shoes by the Door* is a precious gift."

—Greg Boyd, senior pastor, Woodland Hills
Church, Maplewood, Minnesota; author of *Is
God to Blame?* and *Letters from a Skeptic*

"Judi Merriam's poignant book about her son's untimely death stands as a tribute to a mother seeking answers from God, the author of life. Judi does not mince words; her painful journey through years of grief will bring a measure of solace to those who suffer similar tragedies . . . A must-read for all who experience similar tragedies, and those who want to know how best to care for someone who has lost a loved one to suicide.

—Susan Warden Groh, on staff with Navigators
in First Responder ministry, author of *Beauty
Instead of Ashes*, retired pastor's wife who
continues to minister in North Carolina

"A powerful quote from CS Lewis says, 'We read to know we are not alone.' This is the gift at the heart of this book—to those shattered by the loss of a child to suicide, they will find themselves less alone, because someone who has walked this searing road has had the courage to share their story and their honest, broken heart. And in so doing, allowed us to see how offering one's crushed, broken heart to the world is part of the path back to life."

—Joan Horgan, director of spiritual life at the
College of Saint Rose, Albany, New York

EMPTY
SHOES
BY THE
DOOR

EMPTY SHOES BY THE DOOR

— Living —
After My Son's Suicide

A Memoir

JUDI MERRIAM

JAR PRESS

Copyright © 2022 Judi Merriam

All rights reserved.

No part of this book may be reproduced, or stored in a
retrieval system, or transmitted in any form or by any means,
electronic, mechanical, photocopying, recording, or otherwise,
without express written permission of the publisher.

Published by JAR Press, Schenectady

Edited and designed by Girl Friday Productions
www.girlfridayproductions.com

Cover design: Emily Weigel
Project management: Dave Valencia
Editorial: Bethany Davis
Image credits: cover photo of Jenson's shoes © Kalina Merriam
Logo design: Hail O'Donnell

ISBN (paperback): 979-8-9851349-0-2
ISBN (e-book): 979-8-9851349-1-9
LCCN: 2022901977

This book is dedicated to Brian, Tyler, and Kalina, the living, breathing treasures of my heart, and to each and every memory of my beloved Jenson.

November 5, 1993–December 23, 2011

"Who is the happiest of men? He who values the merits of others, and in their pleasure takes joy, even though 'twere his own."

—Jenson's yearbook quote, from *The Poems of Goethe* by Johann Wolfgang von Goethe

Songs are often my greatest means of communication. My days hum with melodies, and song lyrics pop into my head at various and sundry times throughout myriad moments from sunrise to sunset. I especially love musical theater and the joy performing has brought to my life. Therefore, my chapter titles are from a variety of shows I've been in or songs I've sung throughout my lifetime. The musicals in which these songs appear are listed at the end of this memoir.

CONTENTS

"How Could I Ever Know?"

Life is so very different from what I thought it would be. It's fragile and amazing and terrifying and broken and glorious and devastating all at the same time, and it can change in a matter of seconds. A breath can continue a life, or a breath can end a life. Sometimes the ending of a life or the continuing of a life comes down to a choice that should not be ours to make.

On the afternoon of December 23, 2011, the sweetest, kindest, most loving, endlessly creative, intelligent, thoughtful, and polite young man I've ever known died by suicide and robbed my world of one of my most precious treasures. He's my son, Jenson; my second-born, blue-eyed, smiling eighteen-year-old. My life hasn't been the same since he left this earth, and it will never be the same again while I'm still here.

This is my story of Jenson, his life, his death, and how I've survived without his physical presence throughout my days since he died. I write this so I'll never forget who he was and who I am because of him. I write so others will understand who and what I lost on that day Jenson chose to end his life. I write because he wrote, and it seems a fitting way to tell my chosen details of the intriguing, complex, brilliant, and fine young man he was and what my survival has looked like. Jenson was a master weaver of stories and loved the written word in a most passionate way. Stories were the cornerstone of his creativity, whether in written form or in film.

This isn't my husband Brian's story, or my daughter Kalina's story, or my oldest son Tyler's story; it's mine, and I'm telling it the way I think it should be told. More than anything, though, I want you to know that while I take so much time to speak of only one of my dear children, this by no means lessens the great love and admiration I have for my other two, or my husband. I am, most frequently, their biggest champion when challenging those who would challenge them. I would willingly lay down my life for any one of these dear ones in the nucleus of my present soul-cluster of four. They are my treasures, my heartbeats, my DNA of love and commitment. If you ever get to meet my amazing family, it will be a good day for you.

As I share the many happenings of life since Jenson's suicide, I ask you not to judge my extended family or any other people mentioned in these pages. I don't believe anyone who shows up in this book proposed to be clueless or thoughtless in their behavior or the things they said, if indeed they appear that way. In our humanness, we're often incredibly ignorant in our responses to the hurting people in our lives, especially if we haven't experienced that same hurt ourselves.

I've certainly had my own moments of stupendous stupidity when it comes to the words that have come out of my mouth in the past—or still do. However, I truly hope I've learned to be far more wordly-wise and gracious than in my younger years, though I know how easy it is for our mouths to speak in advance of our brains advising, "Stop and think before this leaves your lips."

Most people do the best they can with the pain of others. Some just aren't good at entering into the messiness of life outside their own limited world. I don't, for a second, believe any of the people of whom I write chose willingly to add more hurt to our lives, even when they did. When I share upsetting things that have been said and done in the years since Jenson's death, it's so you may learn and mindfully opt for a more kindly and grace-filled way when you walk with the brokenhearted.

I also write because I'm what those champions who tirelessly and actively work in the field of suicide prevention and education now call a "suicide survivor," and I want you to know what that looks like. With an excruciating amount of hard work, a mind-numbing volume of tears, and a very large amount of time, I've survived Jenson's suicide. It's been an arduous journey; none of it has been easy or simple. I daresay recovery from a suicide death never is, for those left behind.

And just so you're aware of other proper terminology now, the phrase "committed suicide" is no longer used in suicide-awareness dialect and literature. "Committed" sounds like a crime, and in spite of what the law might state, those of us who survive a loved one's suicide do not consider it such. The acceptable terminology is now "completed suicide" or "suicided," so I request you work on leaving the word "committed" out of your discussions when someone dies by their own hand.

Madeleine L'Engle tells us we're all broken, but she says that really isn't a terrible thing. Instead, she states, "Refusing to admit it is what is terrible."[1]

In Psalm 51, King David sang, "The sacrifices of God are a broken spirit. A broken and contrite heart, O God, you will not despise."

I readily admit I'm a broken creature, a broken woman, a broken wife, and a broken mother, and I love the fact that God doesn't despise me for this. Instead, He wraps His loving arms around me and holds me even more tightly because of the fractures in my own humanity.

"We are all broken. That's how the light gets in" is an assumed merged-word quote of phrases from both Ernest Hemingway and Leonard Cohen.[2] I like the saying, no matter who said it, and acknowledge Jesus as the light that gets into my brokenness. I wouldn't be able to write these pages if it weren't for His grace, mercy, and love. Yes, I believe in Him; He's my Savior and my Rescuer, but if I meet you in person, I won't be in your face about this. I greatly dislike when people are in my face about anything, so I try not to do it to others.

Since I'm a woman of faith, Jesus and my faith show up frequently throughout this book. Jesus gives me the ability and wherewithal to put pen to paper. He reminds me of His love for me, for Jenson, and for my present, immediate family of four each time I go back and relive every memory I've included in these pages.

Some of my memories are wonderful, and funny, and special. However, many of them are so excruciatingly painful that I could only write for short periods of time because it hurt too much to write at all. Reliving the pain and heartache was often exhausting and draining. I did it, though, for Jenson, for me, and for those of you reading these words.

I wrote so I could always remember, and so you could see, that no matter what happens in our lives, Jesus is there, already working to bring redemption out of tragedy as He mends the breaches in our hearts and lives. I don't believe God causes tragedy, but I do believe He redeems it.

I often wonder if I'm too dark or negative in what I've written, but I can't answer that question. Sometimes I'm dark; sometimes I'm light; sometimes I'm both at the same time because of the gamut of sensations that go hand in hand while walking through grief and mourning on a daily basis for several years. After tragedy stakes a claim in our lives, grief waxes and wanes like the moon in its journey across the sky. I am whatever I am as I speak the truth of my memory's moments throughout these pages. I imagine it's the same for any of you who may be reeling in the aftermath of whatever has brought grief to your hearts and minds.

I may come across as a woman of negativity, but be patient as you read, for without darkness, there wouldn't be light when the sun rises and morning arrives. Charles Finney tells us not to doubt in the darkness what we know in the light.[3] When truth is spoken, darkness loses its power. We have to move through the darkness in order to inhale relief when the light comes. And when the light comes, we gain a perspective we couldn't see when all was black before our eyes.

I don't hate the darkness, but when it's all there is, my eyes endlessly flutter here and there to find a pinpoint of light—a star, the moon, a glow on the opposite shore, an illuminated window—anything I can fix my eyes on so as to nurture the hope that all is not totally black. Total blackness suffocates the life in my soul, but that pinpoint of light on the horizon tells me darkness is not all there is.

If you want a happy ending according to the world's standards, this isn't the story to read. Although pain and grief aren't all-consuming the way they once were, my family and I continue to walk with them, and I anticipate we will for the rest of our days on this side of Heaven. I suppose it would make everyone feel better if I could say "and we all lived happily ever after," but life isn't a fairy tale, and I refuse to be delusional or live my days in denial.

We can't escape reality no matter how hard we try; it always catches up with us and finds our heart's hiding places. If we don't accept truth early on, grief redefines itself into even greater darkness and devastation. Fairy tales aren't true no matter how many times we cross our fingers or wish upon a star.

I believe truth is typically the best course, so I follow Brené Brown's advice and "rumble" with it, or have a deep conversation with it, regularly, not wanting deception to claim victory. I'm convinced the only healthy way to deal with the factuality of a suicide is to meet it face to face from the heart-wrenching moment it happens and not redefine it into something more acceptable. We also need to personally dictate how we'll deal with it so as to avoid any delusion that would capture our thoughts and change it into something it isn't. It's impossible to dress up a suicide death and be truthful about it at the same time! Some try, but I don't believe them.

I desire that the truth of my own brokenness and survival shines a light on your personal path of grief if you need a pinpoint upon which to fix your eyes and from which to gain encouragement. And I hope this glimpse of one of my fine children allows you a small understanding of what this world lost the day Jenson died, as in the words of Charles Dickens, "And can it be that in a world so full and busy, the loss of one . . . creature makes a void in any heart, so wide and deep that nothing but the width and depth of vast eternity can fill it up?"[4]

PART ONE

CHAPTER 1

"Let's Hear It for the Boy" (Jenson Enters the World)

Secondary infertility loomed large in Brian's and my life together as we waited over three years for a second child. When I discovered I was finally pregnant it was both unexpected and surprising.

Although we hadn't initially wanted to know our baby's gender, near the end of my nine months it was suspected our little one would be a breech birth, so I had to have one last ultrasound. The nurse asked if we wanted to know whether we were having a boy or a girl, and we said yes. Along with pointing out the gender-defining accoutrement, she also disclosed that our upside-down baby had turned himself headfirst for smooth sailing when labor kicked in.

Jenson's due date was smack in the middle of a two-weekend run of a musical I was directing for a local theater company. I made it through every performance only to miss the cast party because I'd given birth the day before. The cast

partied without me; Brian and I were having our own celebration in the hospital.

While all the other laboring mothers were resting quietly
in their delivery rooms after epidurals, I was no-holds-barred
vocalizing Jenson's entrance into the world with my choice of
a completely natural childbirth. One of the nurses actually
told me to try to be quieter so I didn't disturb anyone. Usually
overly thoughtful and considerate, I didn't give a rat's ass about
the other mothers or their comfort level and continued making all the noises necessary to propel my son from the inside
to the outside.

Jenson Edward Merriam entered the world at 12:03 a.m. on
November 5, 1993, when my wailing stopped and his began. As
I held my brand-new son that dismal November morning, he
drank deeply of the first love I offered him, and delight filled
the air. There was no foreshadowing or premonition of any
darkness that lay ahead. Joy abounded, and when joy abounds,
who gives thought to the future? This second son of ours grew,
and joy continued—well . . . sort of.

As long as Jenson could see what lay ahead in his field of
vision he was a pleasant and sweet baby. However, with his
sight line obstructed by the required rear-facing car seat, he
screamed the entire time and distance every time we traveled
by vehicle for the first five months of his life. Nothing would
placate him—not a pacifier, his own thumb, singing to him,
rocking his car seat, or any kind of toy or person in his line of
vision. He finally stopped screaming when he was big enough
to have his seat face forward.

Actually, he may well not have been the exact weight, but
by the time he was remotely close to the correct poundage, we
turned him around simply for our own sanity's sake. Forget safety,
this was about pure, unadulterated survival. His screaming-
Mimi automobile persona came to an instantaneous end
when he could finally see where he was going. In retrospect,

this appeared to be a harbinger of his future every-morning question of "What are we doing today?" which was routinely uttered as soon as he could articulate cohesive thoughts.

Jenson's nature seemed to require from him a constant hankering for knowledge of agendas, plans, and time spans. His desire to know details was understandable; I'm the same way. Could it be genetic, perhaps? Flexibility is not a grace to be enjoyed but an annoyance to endure, especially when others are disorganized and scattered. Jenson was almost always more comfortable with day-to-day living when he knew what lay ahead and what the expectations were. Changes in plans were unnerving for him and left him with a feeling of unsettledness.

From all observations and remembrances, Jenson's childhood seemed fairly normal, as normal goes. Our family did the regular kinds of things others list as healthy—dinners together, a good chunk of "dad-time," fun vacations, lots of educational opportunities, plenty of books and music, time playing outside, time to play with friends, et cetera. Our parenting style was stricter than some but not as strict as that of others we knew when it came to our children's behavior and activities.

We were a homeschool family, but not one that thought our children should always be at home. We purposely chose to live in an urban environment so our children had a much more diverse view of life than what would most likely be found in a middle-class suburban white culture. Our three offspring were well socialized, even to the point of one or two of them occasionally asking, "Can we just stay home?" to which I would respond, "MAY we just stay home?" and then, "No, this activity will be a good experience." I was always on the lookout for good experiences. Isn't that one of the prerequisites for being a good parent?

In my earlier years of mothering, I trained my children well in what I considered the selfless art of "people-pleasing." I was a fine example to them, with my own propensity for trying to be all things to all people, an exhausting and often demeaning task.

If someone talked nonstop to me on the phone for far too long, I wouldn't say, "I need to go now," even though I'd already stopped listening much earlier. The times other mothers wanted me to watch their unruly children, I said, "Okay," even though I greatly disliked those children. When my in-laws and my father said, "You must come to our place on Christmas," I bundled up our kids and drove to too many houses, even though all I wanted to do was stay home. To women who said, "Can my younger children come to Tyler's or Jenson's birthday party, too?" I agreed even though I thought it was incredibly rude of them to ask for younger siblings to take part in the festivities. Saying "yes" was my default response for far too many years.

I later learned it's not "selfless," at all, to agree to what everyone else wants, as my brood and I each struggled to find our own voices in the quest to make the people around us happy. Jenson chose to leave this world before he truly found his voice. Or maybe his leaving was actually the finding of that voice. Who knows?

I also thought I had to be perfect because everyone else appeared to be that way, especially in the homeschool community and in the evangelical church, my choice for worship since age fifteen. Therefore, my house was always spotless when we entertained. It wasn't obvious to me how grumpy I was with my children while accomplishing this task just so our guests would think I had it all together by the time they arrived. After being short-tempered while we cleaned and cooked, I then met our visitors with that hypocritical smile that said "Don't we Merriams look good?" I thought I had to.

My children and I always had to be perfectly attired when we attended church. Every other family was, so that was my standard. But, in my quest to have matching shoes, socks, and outfits, I ignored my peevishness with my family while trying to get out the door to be on time for a service I didn't even want to attend because I didn't think I measured up to everyone else, who had all their children in a nice, neat little row and looked like they were happy to be there. Once we arrived at church I made myself look happy, too. But I wasn't.

When Tyler was in his primary elementary school years, I was too hard on him for not reading as early as practically every other child in our homeschool co-op—whose mothers told me they were reading on a sixth-grade level, or higher, by first grade. I saw Tyler's lack of interest in learning as my failure at not being the perfect homeschool mom, so I took out my frustration on my dear little son. He wanted to play, not read, but I was impatient with him, and at that time had no idea that late bloomers go on to blossom in ways that frequently leave most others in the dust. If only I'd gleaned that knowledge sooner.

I thought my children had to be perfect, too, like everyone else told me their children were. Plus, all the parenting books I read—and I read a lot of them—told me they should be, and if they weren't it was Brian's and my job to change them. In reality, it's hard enough to change myself; why did I ever think I could change my children? And why did I listen to and believe all the voices of people who were just as imperfect as I was?

I glommed onto grace in the earlier years of Jenson's teens and got rid of most of the parenting books I'd read. Jenson celebrated my discovery of grace and probably would've been quite willing to have a book-burning in the backyard had I not chosen to just put them all in the "give-away box" instead. Although, wildly dancing in front of a bonfire of rigid parenting books might have proven far more cathartic than merely passing them off to some other searching soul.

Grace: what a beautiful, glorious word filled with so many promises. I will always be grateful that by the time Jenson died,

I had several years earlier decided to "err on the side of grace" when given the choice. Of course, I'm not always successful, but that's part of the growth process.

I love what Anne Lamott says about this mystical, magical word and God in it: "I do not at all understand the mystery of grace—only that [He] meets us where we are and does not leave us where [He] found us."[5] How exquisite is the truth that God does not leave us where He finds us! What grace is this? What love is this? What mercy is this? Thank you, Lord.

CHAPTER 2

"Farewell, Good Angel" (Jenson Leaves the World)

I held auditions for *Seussical: The Musical* sometime in the second or third week of December 2011. That was the musical I would be directing for the homeschool teens to perform the following spring. I wasn't able to cast Horton from those auditions. I just didn't have a young man who could pull off such a large role. Horton is the lead in the show.

After numerous phone calls to past students, and another round of auditions with some young men who hadn't shown up initially, I still didn't have a Horton. Therefore, I asked my audition committee if they'd be okay with Jenson playing the part, and they unanimously agreed. He would be taking online college classes in his spring semester, so he'd be living at home and available to be in the show. Jenson willingly took the part.

At that time, everything seemed to be falling into place and going really well for him. He finally knew what he wanted to do for the first couple years of college. He'd started dating the young lady he'd been in "love" with since ninth grade. And now he had the lead in a musical he really liked. By all appearances, his life looked rather charmed in December of 2011. Not much seemed wrong in the world of Jenson.

It was also time to gear up for Christmas, and he loved Christmas. He was very particular about the things he wanted for himself, though, and this year was no different, with his lengthy and link-inclusive wish list. I tell you this because it seems to me someone contemplating suicide wouldn't have such a long and concise list of things he hoped to obtain in less than a month. Jenson wasn't one to ask or expect us to waste money on him.

The *Tintin* movie was coming out just before Christmas. *The Adventures of Tintin* is a comics series created by a Belgian cartoonist and was one of the most popular comics of the twentieth century. Jenson had loved *Tintin* since he was a small child. So make this animated series into a movie, and it was a must-see event for my filmmaking son. He organized a large group of friends to go see the movie together and then come back to our house for a party just three days before Christmas.

The afternoon of the party, Jenson went shopping in order to purchase all the needed supplies for the entertaining and feeding of his friends. When he arrived home, he asked us to stay upstairs in our rooms so he could put supplies away and everything would be a surprise. Was he already planning the means of his suicide when he purchased the helium tank and balloons for his evening festivities? Was that why he didn't want us to see what he brought home? As it turned out, the balloons never showed up at that party.

After the movie, several of Jenson's and Kalina's friends came back to our house for snacks, games, and endless talking until around midnight. Our basement was full of laughter, music, and teens coming and going. When the festivities were over, I drove Jenson's girlfriend home while he saw everyone else, save two of his friends, out of the house. Those two friends would spend the night because their mothers couldn't pick them up until the next morning.

When I contemplate reasons for Jenson's suicide, there are some events that flash "perfect storm" in my brain as I ponder their potential for causing a chain reaction of emotional upheaval revolving around his party. Who knows if any of these actually added to an already planned suicide, or were just random coincidences our family looks at as possible impetus behind Jenson's deadly decision. Even though all these are just speculations, in our early days of searching they called out as contributions to the possibility of mounting angst in a highly sensitive eighteen-year-old.

First of all, one of the young men at the party, who was there at my suggestion because he was new to our homeschool co-op, was in everyone's face, physically disruptive, loudly annoying, grabbing items out of people's hands, interrupting almost all conversations, forcing himself into games already begun, and more. He was basically out of control and making Jenson's girlfriend very uncomfortable. This was greatly upsetting to my son, and the next morning he told me he didn't know if he was capable of protecting his girlfriend the way he needed to, which appeared extremely troubling to him.

When Jenson told me this, my thoughts flashed back to the previous night after this young man's mother brought him to the party and then stood on my cellar stairs for almost half an hour telling me unsolicited personal particulars about her life and marriage. I had never met her before, but her information overload followed my simple "Nice to meet you." I wish it had occurred to her, somewhere during her talking my ear off over way too many details of her life, to tell me her son was off-the-wall.

Secondly, one of the two friends who stayed overnight had insomnia and kept Jenson awake the entire time he was there until his mother picked him up at seven thirty a.m. Jenson got absolutely no sleep until that young man went home in the morning. Then he only slept a couple of hours before his best friend's mother came to give her son a ride. At that point, he decided he would just stay up and clean the basement from the party leftovers rather than head to bed for much-needed sleep.

Thirdly, Brian and Jenson were at odds over Jenson wanting to go to a dance rather than the retreat Brian wanted him to attend the same weekend. Brian was still frustrated with Jenson while the party was in full swing and the teens were making noise. They were actually rather quiet as partying teens go, but my husband wanted to sleep and couldn't. He finally got out of bed around one a.m. and, after throwing harsh words at Jenson, left in a huff to go to his office.

And lastly, the morning after the party, I gave Jenson and Kalina a hard time about Kalina and her friends playing "soda pong" the night before. I was so concerned about getting flak from uptight homeschool parents about how "soda pong" looked and sounded like "beer pong" that I wasn't gracious with them when they told me about the game.

I so wish I could have that morning back and say many things differently. Here are the words I would speak instead of what did, or didn't, come out of my mouth.

To Jenson thinking he failed his girlfriend at the party, I would say, "It's really okay, my love; she'll get over it. She needs to be more assertive for herself, anyway, and stop being so overly dramatic about everything. You've now learned to watch out for her a bit more, if need be, and tell someone to 'knock it off' if they're being obnoxious and in your face or her face. It's not rude to do that, especially on your own turf. I'm so sorry I asked you to invite that person to your party. I had no idea how off-the-wall he'd be."

To Jenson thinking about Brian being upset with him and the harsh words that ensued because of it, I would say, "Your dad will get over his tiff. He always does. The three of us will talk about it later today after his office party. You can apologize for the teens being noisy, and I'll apologize for setting off the car alarm under the bedroom window when I got home after taking your girlfriend home. We can also talk about going to the dance rather than the retreat, and we'll figure that out, too. I think it will all be okay after we talk."

To "soda pong" I would have said, "That sounds like a really fun game to play. Did you win every time, Kalina? I bet you did. Ha, ha, ha, wait until the uptight moms call me about that game. Let's see, what shall I say to them when they do? How about 'Why don't you blow it out your big, saggy rear end' [from the movie *RV*]? That would be great fun to say but probably not acceptable if I want to keep their teen in the musical. Hmm, I'll have to think of something more appropriate. I'm not concerned, though, I can handle uptight moms. I've been doing that for years."

But I didn't say any of these things, so I live with regret.

Instead of saying a whole boatload of heartening words to make Jenson realize life was still worth living, I ignored the sound of his angst. Instead of feeling joy because my children had a fun evening with friends the previous night, I was steeling myself for phone calls from mothers who were even more uptight than I was.

What an exhausting way to live. Because I wasn't regularly afforded grace by some of the overly conservative mothers in the homeschool community, I didn't consistently extend grace to my own children as much as I should. Jenson's death day would be one of my graceless legacy memories for the rest of my life; if only I'd nailed grace before my children were even born.

Brian's office Christmas party was that afternoon, and Jenson, Kalina, and I were all invited. It was to include bowling and pizza at a local bowling alley. My present reality is that I've neither stepped inside that bowling alley nor gone bowling again since that day. Bowling brings memories of death, which may not change, and at this time, I see no need to work through this particular disquietude.

In his book *Flatbellies*, Alan B. Hollingsworth says something similar to "Perseverance is simply continuing to walk with a knife in your heart."[6] There are times when that heart-knife is so much more painful and unnecessary than others, so those are the moments I choose to avoid in order to continue functioning.

Jenson didn't want to go to the office party and chose to stay home. Did he already know why he was staying home—to kill himself? What was going through his head when he said "goodbye" to Kalina and me as we walked out the door and left? He always hugged me and told me he loved me whenever I left the house. That day was no different. At least we shared a hug and our love before I never saw him again.

In hindsight I do believe he looked sadder than usual, but I only thought how tired he must really be from staying up all night. It's amazing to me how sometimes we can miss something that might be there, while other times we're certain we've noticed something that really isn't what we think it is. There is so much fallibility in being human, and yet we expect perfection from ourselves and practically everyone else in our lives. There's no grace in that.

How could Jenson let us go out that door knowing he'd never see us again? What were his thoughts as he watched us walk away? Had he already made the choice to go back to his bedroom to take his life? What were the exact series of events that followed Kalina's and my departure before Jenson executed his plan for his own leaving? We'll never know.

I so wish I'd insisted he go to the party with us even though he didn't want to go and might well have had a lousy attitude. If I'd forced him to go with us, would he still be alive or would he have just opted out on a different day? The legacy of a suicide is the list of never-ending, mind-numbing "what ifs" playing on a continuous loop in the deliberations of survivors.

Brian's office party ended before five p.m., and he and Kalina headed home while I went shopping for food and last-minute Christmas items. While I was in the grocery store, Brian called and asked, "What time will you be home to make supper?"

I responded, "I'm almost done at the grocery store, and then I have one more stop to make before I come home."

"Okay, I'm kind of hungry, though, so hopefully you'll be home soon."

After ending our phone call, my brain rambled, "That's odd he's hungry considering all we ate at his office party. He's never called before to ask when I'm going to make supper. What's up with that? Wow, he sounded really tired." These were all just passing thoughts, though, so I gave a mental shrug and continued with my shopping, attributing the phone call to his having been awake for over twenty-four hours. It didn't occur to me that anything was amiss. Why would it?

When I arrived home, a crime-scene van was parked in front of our house. However, I was still completely heedless of the possibility that anything might have happened in my home. Brian met me at the door, and I jokingly asked, "Why is that van out front?" Then I looked at his face as he said, "I have something to tell you." How quickly our smiles turn to imminent screams.

I could feel a sense of panic spread throughout my body like the feverish warmth from standing too close to a fire. I demanded he tell me what happened, but he wanted me to sit down first. I refused and just kept repeating over and over with rising volume, "Tell me what happened," as he led me into our living room.

Brian then said, "Jenson's dead. He took his life." I saw his mouth moving, but the words coming out made no sense. It was seconds before those words took on meaning in my per-plexed brain.

When I was a teenager I heard the scream of a rabbit as it flew through the night sky captured in the talons of an owl. It was the most terrifying sound I've ever heard in my life.

I recognized that same animalistic shriek as it came from the depths of my bowels in the shape of "NO," sounding over and over again. It wouldn't stop as I frantically paced back and forth holding on to my head to stop it from exploding. That shriek drove me to my knees and then prostrate on the floor, where it morphed into a desperate cry of "My God, my God, why have you forsaken us" as I rolled back and forth, pounding fists into carpet. If Hell is truly separation from God, that was where I landed, demoralized and severed from my Savior.

"Why is it that we yell 'No,' knowing good and well how useless it is? Do we think if we yell it loud enough that God will listen? Or is it so we can't hear the horrible sound of our own hearts breaking?"[7] The realization that Jenson had taken his life was the singularly most devastating thing that had ever touched my heart, and in those first moments of knowing, I was certain God had abandoned and forsaken me forever.

Eventually I pulled my face out of the carpet and rose from the floor, firing questions at Brian. He answered with: "Jenson used a plastic bag and the helium tank he purchased for his party to asphyxiate himself." "The crime-scene van is still here because officers are up in Jenson's bedroom looking over everything and assessing his death." "Tyler and Kalina are on their way home; they went for a ride so I could tell you what happened." I tried to make sense of what he was telling me, but all I could comprehend was the sobbing that must have been mine.

Tyler and Kalina arrived home, and the four of us huddled together, trying to will comfort upon ourselves and each other, but no comfort came. We finally sat down so they could all tell me what had transpired before I arrived home. What they had to say would break my heart even more because of what each of them had to go through without me there to help.

Tyler had traveled home from graduate school late that afternoon, and since no one greeted him when he came through the front door, he assumed we were all at Brian's office party. He had absolutely no reason to think anything was wrong. It never occurred to him to call out to anyone or check bedrooms. Jenson's was on the third floor, anyway, and if he was home, he would have heard Tyler and come down to be with him. Tyler was Jenson's hero.

Brian and Kalina arrived home around five p.m., and Kalina sensed something was wrong the minute she entered the front door. More specifically, she said she knew Jenson was dead, but didn't verbalize it to her father or oldest brother. Instead, she went up to his bedroom and found the door locked. He almost always left his door open during the day so his room would be warmer with the rising heat. To our knowledge, Jenson had never, ever locked his door in the past. There was no need to do so.

Kalina told Brian that Jenson's door was locked and he wouldn't answer when she knocked or called to him. Brian finally found a skeleton key that would open the door, so they unlocked it and went in. When they entered the room, Brian was confused about what he saw. Reality finally sank in and he yelled for Tyler and told Kalina to call 911 while he began CPR on Jenson. Tyler and he took turns trying to revive their brother and son, but it was too late.

No parent or sibling should ever have to see their child or brother dead by his own hand, or anyone else's for that matter, but that's the vision Brian, Tyler, and Kalina have to live with for the rest of their lives. In their mind's eye, they will always have that picture of Jenson dead on the floor. That will be their last visual memory of him. For weeks after, Brian would sob and talk about that scene. Tyler and Kalina would hold their grief and pain more privately, which I found even more tragic.

Kalina later told me she's grateful Jenson didn't take his life by some other means that would have been even more devastating for us, his family. She thinks Jenson planned his method of death as a kindness out of his love for us. A helium-tank/plastic-bag death is quick and clean. There's no blood, no mess, nothing to wash afterward, and no physical marks on a body.

How ludicrous is it that we think this is a kindness to us? How absurd that we would be grateful for an easy cleanup? How ridiculous is it that the word "glad" would be used in talking about Jenson's method of suicide?

In addition to already feeling guilty about not rectifying things with Jenson before Brian left for work early that morning, his guilt would intensify for not praying over Jenson's body and asking God to intervene and bring him back to life. Brian and Tyler were so intent on their CPR, Brian didn't think to pray.

Do other people really think to do that when they're in the midst of trying to physically save a child? Another friend of mine, whose son took his life, would say the same thing to me years later: Why didn't she or her pastor pray to bring that son back to life? There are no answers to that question, but it seems to me God is big enough to have put that thought into a mind if it were an option for life to continue. This is part of the residual parental guilt of our child's suicide: "Why didn't we . . . ?" We ask it over and over and over again, especially during the rawness of the first few years after death.

Before leaving our house, the police officer came and told us that because there was no suicide note, they suspected foul play. There *was* a note, though, and Brian had it in his pocket. He'd read that note to me earlier, and my thoughts were "That doesn't sound like something Jenson would write to us. It sounds cold and detached. Jenson's notes are always loving and kind and detailed." It was in Jenson's handwriting, though, so he must have written it. How could he have written something that didn't sound like his own words?

> JENSON'S SUICIDE NOTE: *Time to go. Totally not anyone's fault, I promise. Just, I now know that I can't be what I need to be. I love you, Mom, Dad, Kalina, and Tyler. And I really do love you, [girlfriend's name], with all my heart. C'est la vie! Peace Out.*

The police left with my sweet Jenson in a body bag. I'd seen body bags countless times in crime shows on TV, but how could there possibly be one leaving my own safe, peaceful, loving household? Body bags belonged in movies, sitcoms, and fictional stories, not in the homes and lives of real people who loved and cherished each other. It just couldn't be possible Jenson was leaving our house that way.

The house was now empty of everyone but the four of us and seemed void of any sound save the all-consuming pounding anguish in our hearts and minds. We couldn't stand the misery of being alone with ourselves, so we called our pastor. He and his wife would come over as soon as they could get there, so we waited, lost in our individual and communal brokenness.

I'll always wonder if Tyler felt more guilt than the rest of us during the silent moments of that evening. He shared with us that he thought Jenson would've told him if something was wrong, since he was the safest family member for Jenson. Jenson knew he could trust Tyler with any information, and Tyler wouldn't overreact or be judgmental.

Yet nothing had been said or shared to cause Tyler any speculation over Jenson's well-being. He told us Jenson Facebook-messaged him that very morning to say he could hardly wait for Tyler to arrive home later that day so they could spend their Christmas vacation together. Why would Jenson write that if he knew he'd be dead by the time Tyler entered our house? Was it just a ruse on Jenson's behalf, a fine acting job so as to belie his plans for the day? Why would he do that to a brother he loved and admired so very much?

Kalina didn't want to sleep at home, so her best friend's mother came to pick her up and take her to their house. It's interesting the things I remember from those first shock-filled hours after Jenson's death. One of the things so vivid in my mind is that mother hugging me when she arrived at our house. I felt claustrophobia rise with the intensity of that hug and wanted to run and hide. She was being so very loving, as she and her family deeply cared for Jenson, and yet the last thing I seemed to want was to be touched.

For days afterward everyone would want to hug or touch me because they needed it for themselves and probably thought it would bring me comfort. It didn't bring me comfort, though, and my anxiousness grew with people's lingering emotional embraces. Perhaps it was somehow related to the initial feelings of a constricted heart, the inability to draw breath, and the feeling that the world had ended and chaos reigned after Brian first told me of Jenson's suicide.

Our pastor and his wife finally arrived and stayed with us late into the night. This would be our pastor's gift to us, his compassion and help in this time of crisis. Not everyone is good at that, but I can't imagine anyone else walking with us as tenderly as our pastor did through that first evening or the next couple of days. When they arrived, all we did was talk and cry and wonder and question—always the questions.

Why would Jenson take his life? What was so terrible to cause him to make that choice? What did he think he needed to be? What did he think we wanted him to be? Was he gay and couldn't tell us? Was he dreading his college and career choices? Was it because Brian had given him a hard time about not going to a retreat? Was he mentally ill, and we'd been clueless about it? Was he greatly depressed, and we'd been oblivious to that? Had his girlfriend broken up with him? Had he broken up with his girlfriend? What did it mean, it was his time to go? And on, and on, and on . . .

It was surreal, as if I were watching that scene in the living room from outside my own body. "There I am on the couch, but how can I be a part of this reality of Jenson's death; it all has to be a nightmare. But I can't seem to wake up to get away from what I'm seeing. So I must already be awake, but how can I be if this doesn't feel real? Am I here watching this, or am I there living it?" The talons of horror wouldn't release me, so I forced myself back into my body sitting in the living room no matter how much I didn't want to be in that actuality.

I can't say enough about how loving and kind Tyler was that evening. His pain must have been just as unbearable as Brian's and mine, and yet he was there with us, a devoted presence in our suffering. He would continue to do anything he could for us throughout the rest of his Christmas break at home. Tyler has honed the fine skill of listening and just sitting with people as needed without giving opinions or platitudes, a gift indeed.

I'm afraid, though, we weren't thinking enough about Tyler's and Kalina's broken hearts. Parents get a great deal of attention when a child dies, but siblings are often left to fend for themselves as they walk through their own personal pain. There are numerous articles and books written to support and encourage parents who are dealing with the loss of a child, but siblings are typically overlooked. Tyler's unselfish investment of devotion to us at that time, and Kalina's extreme kindness, were astounding gifts. My children are treasures indeed.

When the first morning after Jenson's death arrived, following an onerous night never seeming to end, it brought an endless number of people coming into and going out of our

house. For several days, there would be no time when we were
home alone other than to sleep at night.

As more and more people found out about Jenson, the
amount of people coming to our door increased, as did phone
messages to our voice mail, emails to our computer screens,
and posts to Brian's, Tyler's, and Jenson's Facebook pages.
Only once did I feel even a hint of condemnation from anyone who contacted us, from one man the day after the twenty-
third. Everyone else was loving, kind, and supportive beyond
imagining.

Christmas arrived two days after Jenson took his life, and
we decided to get up and open presents in some attempt at
normalcy for Tyler and Kalina. We smiled at each other and
passed presents around, but it was all in trance-like shock.
Jenson's presents, from him and for him, were under the tree.
Opening his presents to us, we stared at them as we held them
in our hands, looking for him so we could declare an enthusiastic "Thank you, I love it." But his face was nowhere to be
found, so our lips closed in dismay. His unopened presents created a pile of regret that would define Christmas for the rest of
our lives. That pile needed to go to his room so we didn't have
to look at it.

We went through the motions of a celebration, but there's
almost no memory of it; we all seemed to carry an inner dead-
ness ourselves. It would take many years of Christmases before
that dead feeling would leave me on that particular holiday. I
still don't like Christmas the way I did before 2011. There is
always an intense sense of relief when it's over and we're past
that celebratory date so close to Jenson's suicide remembrance.

Our pastor and his wife stopped to see how we were
before they left for a week in Tennessee with their own family.
Another couple came by to smile and share pleasantries; the
husband was encouraging, the wife just stood there dressed
in her discomfort. I think my sister dropped in at some point,

but she had her partner's family to entertain and didn't want them to know about our loss and ruin their Christmas, so she didn't stay. Did anyone else come to the door for greetings? I don't remember.

Later that day the two men who would help us break into Jenson's computer, a very good friend of Jenson's and his father, would arrive to continue working along with Brian and Tyler on the difficult task of figuring out how to get into masterfully protected writings. These men had given us a large amount of time on Christmas Eve, too, a generous gift when being with family is so expected. We needed them to find *something* for us, because Jenson's suicide note was not defining enough for us to say, "Now we know why."

At some point later that day, they were finally able to break into Jenson's files, and we found three different things he'd written hinting at possible unrest in his heart. One of those writings was titled "The Art of Suicide." *What?* "The Art of Suicide"? What could that possibly mean? I couldn't bear for us to read any of those writings on Christmas Day, so we left them unopened and waited until Monday, when a different caring-pastor would be with us and we wouldn't have to sit alone.

I didn't know if any of us could keep body and soul together during the reading of Jenson's writings. I was sure there'd be tangible reasons for us to say, "This is why he took his life." In my mother-guilt screaming louder than normal in my head during those early after-suicide days, I supposed we'd learn how we had somehow failed him and why he was, therefore, dead by his own hand.

So come Monday morning, after that dazed Christmas Sunday, all but Kalina sat at our kitchen table with our pastor friend. I held my breath in dread for what seemed like the entire time Tyler read Jenson's words out loud to us, but there was nothing. *Nothing* he wrote hinted at or gave us a clue as to his motive for ending his life. I allowed myself to breathe as Tyler set the papers down on our kitchen table, and we all stared at each other.

Later, I would take those writings to both of our grief counselors and ask their opinions about them. They would each admit there were no blatant red flags that would give rise to suspicion about Jenson's intent. One would be a bit more apprehensive, but not overly enough to say, "Oh, now I see why." My counselor would even say Jenson's "The Art of Suicide" sounded like the title for a bad English assignment rather than a statement about his mental well-being. She would go on to say he wrote extremely well, with no hint or suggestion of apparent psychological issues, whatsoever.

We were no further ahead with any particular motive than we had been before that Monday we'd read Jenson's password-protected files. At this time, though, acceptance was still not an option, because his "It's time for me to go" in a suicide note was not an adequate explanation for his choice.

We wanted reasons, so it was for reasons we were continuously searching. It would be a very long time before that endless probing would look anything like resignation. Our desperate search for answers continued for months upon months.

I'm not sure if people can truly see a foreshadowing of their future. Jenson had a discerning mind, and that, combined with his sensitive heart, may well have allowed him to be more in tune with his past, present, and future than other people might be. When Brian and I would attempt a serious discussion about what he wanted to do after high school, he would often get upset and sometimes even cry.

This was a typical pattern for him no matter what the atmosphere or his mood before the conversation. It was a bit mystifying, because we didn't feel as if we were being harsh or presumptuous. We were just trying to help him make some decisions that needed to be made so he didn't spend his entire life holed up in his bedroom on his computer, even if he was being creative with his writing and filmmaking.

Brian and I have pondered the possibility he somehow knew he didn't have a long future and therefore couldn't talk about it; if so, what a terrible burden to bear alone at such a young age. If that was a possible likelihood, I've wondered how long he might have felt that way, what his true thoughts were about such, and if he was fearful about what lay ahead.

Nevertheless, Jenson was gone and we couldn't stay within the walls of our house forever. We had to figure out what our own futures would look like. There was paperwork to address, decisions to make, Jenson's room to go through and organize, people to talk to, commitments needing follow-through, a counselor to find, daily life to be lived—the list seemed endless and overwhelming in the midst of shock.

So whatever the next thing was that needed doing, that was what we did as we stepped into 2012 and a future without one of our children.

PART TWO

CHAPTER 3

"Before the Parade Passes By" (Support)

The Merriam side of the family vacationed together in Ocean Isle, North Carolina, when Jenson was about six or seven years of age. We all spent a huge amount of time on the beaches, swimming, playing games, and building sandcastles. Some family members decided to combine their artistic talents with burying each other in the sand. Jenson and his closest cousin, born the same year he was, decided to allow themselves to be buried, while others created elaborate mermaid/merman bodies of sand around their seated torsos. The artwork detail was actually quite spectacular.

Being buried in the sand is not for the faint of heart. The combination of water suction and lack of mobility can be rather traumatizing for those who don't like the impediment of body movement. Jenson's cousin started to panic and cry out in fear. The two of them were positioned next to each other, so he merely reached out and took her hand. That simple gesture of comfort worked, and the crying stopped. Jenson reached out in love, and even though his cousin's circumstances didn't change, the act of consolation was all that was needed to calm her breath and stay her tears.

We were flooded with countless acts of consolation ourselves, especially cards, beginning the day after Jenson's death. Cards arrived for weeks upon weeks, some from people I didn't even know. What treasures they were, but I couldn't focus on them in the wake of the sheer volume we received. I saved every single one so I could read through them again at a later date when my brain wasn't so stultified by stupor. I really wanted to pay attention to what was said to us, about us, about Jenson, and about God, but it would be several months before I was able to do that.

I'm grateful for all the lovely encouraging personal words written to us, and I'm glad I kept them to read a second time when the words actually made sense to a brain that was no longer sheltered by shock. Now, when I send cards to those in the throes of a loved one's loss of life, I wait a bit until time has sanded off some of that first morbid edge of death. I figure my own words might be more valuable later than sooner.

I also greatly appreciated cards arriving at random times for a few years after Jenson's death. Not only did cards occasionally come on days like Mother's Day, Jenson's birthday, and his death date but some people would remember to email me at specifically difficult times, too. It took effort and determination to do that by remembering which dates might be painful for my hurting mother-heart. Some continue to do this, even now. These treasures-to-my-heart friends know the pain never ends, no matter how many years have passed.

We decided to have a memorial service for Jenson rather than a funeral and calling hours. How or why that decision was made escapes my memory, but at the time it seemed like the right thing to do. His body had been cremated, and the thought of having a wake and funeral seemed overwhelmingly depressing. A memorial service appeared more life-giving than death-magnifying in our circumstances, to us the natural thing to do. We so needed to focus on Jenson's life, because all we could see was his death at that time.

The service was set for January 7, 2012, two weeks after he died. That date was chosen so we had time to plan, our pastor would be back from his Christmas holiday, and Jenson's college friends could attend before going back to school. Our pastor visited us the week before in order to talk about how the service would go. He'd invited the pastor who took care of us the week after Christmas to also speak and be a part of our ministrations on the seventh.

As we discussed details, our pastor proposed that one of the women from our church sing. Brian and I both responded with a resounding and distinct "No" followed by me saying, "I'm going to sing." Our pastor and his wife thought this a poor choice, speculating that it would be too emotional for me and I wouldn't actually be able to make it through a song.

It was something I needed to do, though, and they could not budge me from my decision. I assured them I'd also find my own singer to stand in if I wasn't able to follow through with the song. I was adamant about this. It was our Jenson's memorial service, and I wasn't about to be talked out of something so very important to me. If I did nothing else, I had to sing; my deepest pain and joy are manifested through song.

Thankfully, there was no snow on that Saturday of Jenson's service. I don't even remember if it was sunny or not, but I do remember there was no snow, a mercy indeed. All of Brian's and my extended family members were there. I wish I could say they felt like a fortress of love and support, but that wasn't the case. I still felt like Brian, Tyler, Kalina, and I were completely on our own in our grief.

When it was time for the service to begin, we left the shelter of the pastor's study and began walking out to sit in our seats. All breath left me upon my first glimpse of the sanctuary; my body called out to collapse as I stared at the multitude of people filling that space. My feet refused to continue forward as my thoughts called out in my head, "Dear God, I've got to run back to the office and escape all this." But Jenson's girlfriend's mother said, "Just breathe," and propelled me forward.

Every inch of the sanctuary and balcony was packed with people. Extra chairs had to be set up in front of the pews and in the narthex. Never before had I seen that space hold so many bodies. There were church friends, theater friends, Jewish friends, Rotary friends, homeschool friends, friends of Tyler and Kalina, community friends, college friends, work friends, music friends, music teachers, old friends, young friends, new friends, politicians, students, friends not seen in years, coworkers, bikers, and more. What a compilation of people from every facet of our combined family and personal lives. It was mind-boggling.

I recognized some faces, but others were a blur in a sea of compassionate humanity who came to remember Jenson and support us in our loss. We were told there were over a thousand people at that memorial service. How could that be? How could there be that many people who cared about Jenson and us? How could that many people want to be there in spite of the way Jenson died? How could he not have known how loved he was? How could we not know how loved we were? We walked to our seats, sat down, and the service began.

My memory can't seem to recover much of what was said by the two pastors that afternoon. We have a recording of the service, but I've never listened to it; I haven't wanted to, even all these years from that date. Brian and I had been adamant that we wanted the pastors to assure those in attendance that we knew Jenson was in Heaven and suicide was not the unpardonable sin some believe it is.

We sang a couple of hymns before those of us who were to speak had our say. Kalina's cello teacher would later tell me, "I've never in my life heard a congregation sing like that before, with all those combined voices. It was absolutely amazing to hear that many people filling the church with their volume, melodies, and harmonies. I don't think I'll ever forget what they sounded like. I don't want to ever forget what they sounded like. It was quite heavenly."

I wish I'd been aware enough to really listen. My guess is if I had, the sheer magnitude of all those voices would have brought me a goodly amount of comfort, but I can't hear any of that singing in my memory. Too bad; I would love a touch of "heavenly" to pull out of the recesses of my mind about that day. Perhaps I should listen to the recording.

I also don't recall being consoled or agitated by what was spoken out of the mouths of the pastors or my father-in-law at that service. I only remember when Brian and Tyler spoke I found their words extremely cogent, loving, and articulate considering the loss their hearts were holding. My own pain intensified over their suffering and the sting of death.

I spoke last in order to sing when done. My dear friend Kate sat behind me, willing me to sing but ready to take my place if emotions disallowed me to continue. My chosen song was "Blessings" by Laura Story. It was the one song seeming to speak words I needed to both hear and sing that day. It was also the only time in my entire life I remember not feeling nervous standing in front of an audience. Jenson consumed my attention, and I cared nothing for what those listening thought of me or my voice.

Looking out into the crowd as I sang, I recognized a few faces, and though some were smiling, they still looked so very sad. However, nothing really registered in my mind other than the lyrics leaving my mouth. It was like singing to a screen of faces that weren't really alive in front of me, almost as if someone had dropped a veil that clouded the clarity of those sitting in the pews. I made it through the song before grief claimed my vocal cords on the final notes. Walking to my seat, I exhaled the tears I'd been holding back.

On a later day, a few weeks down the road, one of Brian's employees would tell me he'd never heard me sing so beautifully. How odd that may well have been my reality on such a poignant day; I hope it's true. "Blessings" was my sacrificial gift to both Jenson and God, streaming from a heart broken by love.

We hadn't given thought to or planned for what would happen immediately after the memorial service other than our own church ladies providing food in the fellowship hall for people who might want to eat. Since we'd never even contemplated the number of people in attendance, it didn't occur to us what might transpire if they all stayed to see us after the service. There wasn't any discussion about directly talking to everyone other than our need to protect Kalina from the hugging and touching she so hated if people sought her out.

It in no way entered our minds what to do once we left the sanctuary. We certainly hadn't anticipated greeting one thousand people; we'd only been expecting two hundred or so. It never dawned on us people would want to stay after and talk to us. Why would they want to do that? Jenson took his life; wouldn't they prefer to avoid us? Isn't that what usually happens with a suicide—avoidance?

To our utter astonishment, about seven hundred of those who came to the service joined us in the fellowship hall afterward. These loving and kind people formed a line so they could all take turns greeting us. That line snaked its way around the room with no end in sight. We greeted people for over four hours.

I hadn't even smiled as much or hugged as many people at our wedding, and that had been a day of joy. How was it I was still smiling at people and thanking them for their love for four hours on a day memorializing such death and loss? Shock is the answer. Shock is always the grace that allows people to survive through early days of devastation and desperation.

By the time the last of those people left, I was totally devoid of any emotion, thought, or energy. My smile was just a plaster cast by then. We'd been at church since noon or so, and it was now almost nine p.m. How we survived that day is still astounding to me, but as William Ritter says, "the same arms that catch the dying also carry the living."[8] We were carried by God's mercy and grace and the love of all who showed up to walk through that service with us. Gratitude intermingled with my pain at that realization.

It might be very encouraging if I could tell you that the over one thousand people who attended that service are still a loving, supportive, and caring network in our lives, but that's not true, nor do I want it to be. It would be overwhelming to regularly interact with that number of people, so this is not a criticism of anyone. I will always be extremely grateful for those who gave us the gift of their time and support that day. I don't, at all, wish to diminish the presence of any who loved us enough to show up two weeks after Jenson's suicide.

I doubt many had ever been to a memorial service for someone who died by their own hand before that. It was probably very difficult for much of the crowd who came, and I'm honored they made the choice to do so. I have no desire to lessen anyone's love for us or legacy of pain at Jenson's loss, no matter where they scattered to after January 7, 2012.

I assume most moved on with their own lives after they'd spent their personally perceived sufficient amount of time grieving for and with us. Since bad news typically draws a crowd, several moved on to the next crisis that arose after Jenson's suicide. Many stepped out of our lives for good, and because silence is almost always misinterpreted, their with-drawal from our contact was easier for both them and us.

These are neither judgmental nor critical statements but merely observations of people in general. Humans often have a short attention span when it comes to the bereavement of others; it simply seems to be our nature to not sit well with sorrow for long periods of time. Callousness is not my intention with this statement, just my conclusion since December of 2011.

Before Jenson died I most likely moved on quickly, too, especially when someone appeared better than they may actually have been. But now I understood what Jill Kelly so aptly describes with her words: "a relentless, hollow ache echoes through every part of my broken life, and it will until heaven . . . a gaping hole once filled with joy is now empty."[9] I now know that emptiness doesn't end.

I honestly don't blame anyone for their questionable behavior toward us in the ensuing months after the memorial service. There are no instruction manuals for how people should walk with others through grief. Grief, in and of itself, is hard, but suicide grief separates the wheat from the chaff when it comes to people's personality propensities for getting down and dirty in the nitty-gritty mess of life and death. It has always surprised me who walked away, who stayed, and who showed up out of nowhere.

I have to admit I don't miss the people who walked away. It's a relief not to have their proclivity for drama in my daily life. I've learned to set boundaries with some of those who stayed but needed parameters so as not to drain me of my hard-won stability. And those who showed up surprised me the most and demonstrated how God's grace works in ways we don't perceive when we can't see beyond the immediate circumstances of our tragedy.

Kalina's annual physical was scheduled for the end of January, a couple of weeks after Jenson's service. Her doctor was in the same practice as Jenson's doctor, the amiable and knowledgeable caregiver who had seen my son since he was born, attended his memorial service, and was so kind to all of us afterward. Jenson liked his doctor a great deal and had just seen him for his eighteenth-year physical at the beginning of December, about two and a half weeks before he elected to leave life.

During Kalina's physical, Jenson's doctor called me into his office. Some of his staff had come out to offer me sympathy after I first arrived and then gone to tell him I was in the waiting area. Sad news travels more quickly than we realize.

This doctor closed his door behind me and asked, "How are you holding up?"

"I guess I'm okay," I said, my normal response during those days of emotional turmoil and upheaval when I honestly didn't know how to answer.

He then explained, "I spent a good chunk of time looking through Jenson's records and rereading everything I'd written down since he was born."

I didn't know if I was expected to say something, but the doctor continued, so I remained silent. "I could find nothing that offered any clue or even hinted at the possibility of him taking his life. As a matter of fact, he'd always been delightful, very healthy, and completely cooperative throughout every one of his doctor visits, even the one a couple of weeks before he died. I never saw any red flags that caused me concern about his mental health."

I could feel a sense of relief slowly begin to pulsate through my body.

"The only thing I can think to tell you is that sometimes the really sensitive souls like Jenson are more susceptible to suicide. I'm just so sorry for his death. He was a fine and wonderful young man."

My relief continued to sound louder than my original concern of being called into his office. What a commodity of comfort his professional words were. What a gift he gave our family by taking the time to both look through his Jenson files, without being asked to do so, and then tell me about finding nothing. This man, who'd seen our son his entire life, had seen no disturbance or angst either. I left his office with a palpable sense of consolation.

Support also came through meals given to us from people at our church and the moms of the *Seussical* cast members. I think our church family brought us meals for at least two months, and the *Seussical* moms brought meals every Friday from January through April. I was filled with thankfulness for these generous gifts of food. With my brain substantially scrambled during the early months of 2012, it was such a relief to not have to think about feeding my family on top of all the other aspects of surviving grief and directing a musical.

Even though our souls and minds were starving for peace and comfort, at least our bodies were being nourished by all that food provided out of love. It's quite amazing how actual physical acts of giving food, cleaning a house, running errands, et cetera, demonstrate love and compassion far more powerfully than words alone. I remain in continual appreciation for those who showed up to do more than speak platitudes.

There are a few precious friends who lovingly hold my grieving heart, mind, and words in a trustworthy way as they continue to support me in my loss, year after year. These women honor Jenson by loving me and reaching out to remember him at random times, or on his birthday or death date. I may not hear from some of these women regularly, but they are always there when my heart is most needy.

There's my sister, who regularly contributes to World Vision, or other organizations, in his memory for Christmas. There's Elisa, who almost never forgets to text me words of love and encouragement on his birthday. MaryAnna, one of my delightful past students, sends me birthday cards for Jenson and contacts me on Mother's Day because she knows that's a hard day for me. Doreen regularly talks with me about my son and gives me yellow roses just because he loved her lemon bars. Melissa consistently remembers Jenson on one of his difficult-for-me memory days every year. There are others, but these are the women who regularly support me on my darkest days of loss.

What's surprising to me, too, are the people who don't know me well and haven't spent much time in my company, but nonetheless contact me at random times simply to ask how I'm doing. What kindness that demonstrates. They don't reach out to analyze or give their opinions, but merely to honestly and compassionately ask how I'm doing.

A woman from whom I took a library writing class is one of those people. Because she contacted me out of the blue, she transformed herself from a teacher to a treasure. When she emailed me after Christmas just to inquire how I was, a couple of years ago, I responded with this: "Grief is often singing in my head, but it's not the all-consuming wail it once was at Christmastime for the first couple of years after my son's death. Hope is a great gift."

Yes, hope is a great gift, but so are the people who ask how we are and allow us to answer honestly while they keep their mouths silent from platitudes or rhetoric. William Ritter reminds us that "the best way to honor the dead is to love the living."[10] I'm so grateful for the people who honor Jenson by loving me.

Something to Consider: I would encourage you readers not to anticipate any kind of response after you've sent a sympathy card, even if you included a beautiful message of love and encouragement. I've heard from other grieving parents about how difficult it was to acknowledge cards, personal notes, and monetary donations after their child died. Parents are doing their best to barely breathe and walk through each day after the death of a child. Throw in caring for the rest of their family and adequately functioning after the shock has worn off, and there may just be no time or energy for the writing of thank-you notes.

Give the grace you would wish to receive if your heart was broken. Everyone has a personal scope of what can or can't be accomplished while walking through grief. Out of necessity, letter writing may well be something that goes right out the door in exchange for survival. Please don't judge a grieving parent by your own standards of personal politeness. Just because a thank-you note isn't sent, or a pre-printed card is, doesn't mean the grieving person is not grateful.

CHAPTER 4

"Bewitched, Bothered, and Bewildered"
(Cleaning Up)

Even though Jenson was generous with his love as he grew out of his preschool years, he was very particular in his preferences toward certain adults. If he loved you, he'd do anything to demonstrate that love. He'd write you little notes, draw you pictures, give his things to you, give his siblings' things to you, and more. I'd regularly ask the adults and children exiting our front door if Jenson had given them anything. If the items belonged to Tyler or Kalina, I would retrieve them and return them to their rightful owners. Perhaps, though, some specific items never found after endless searching actually departed in the pocket of someone on the receiving end of Jenson's generosity. We'll never know.

He particularly loved one of my former students, a regular babysitter of ours for quite a few years. She was getting married, and although Jenson was extremely fond of her husband-to-be, he wasn't pleased about losing the love of his five-year-old life to another man. While in the receiving line after the wedding, he grabbed the bride in a bear hug and stated in a very loud voice so that others, including the new husband, could hear, "You were supposed to marry me." The woman of his dreams was lost to another man, and his little heart was broken by love. He had to figure out how to live with that loss.

Brian's, Tyler's, Kalina's, and my hearts were broken by love, too, way beyond the pain of Jenson's preschool heart losing the woman he wanted to marry, and we had to figure out how to live in and with our own loss. We were crushed by the severity of our bereavement but had to reckon with all the paperwork needing to be addressed in the process of cleaning up after Jenson's suicide.

If there was a *How to Clean Up the Mess Left by Your Child's Suicide* book out there, I never found it, and I spent hours looking. If there was some sort of "cleaning up" pamphlet on suicide prevention and awareness sites, it wasn't evident, and I spent hours searching. If anyone else knew, they didn't tell me, and I spent hours asking. So we were left with no instructions for what to do or how to do it when it came to "what now?" and "what next?"

The second thing that had to be done after deciding on a date for Jenson's memorial service was to come up with his obituary, so I sat down and wrote. It was egregious to me to say he died "suddenly," "tragically," or "unexpectedly." That's what's almost always stated in an obituary when someone takes their own life. My heart's desire was for complete honesty and words that spoke the truth. Therefore, I wrote "Jenson took his own life . . . at his home," finished the rest of the obituary, and emailed it to the funeral home.

The undertaker, a longtime family acquaintance whose children had been in several choirs and musicals I'd directed in earlier years, called to discuss my openness and honesty. Brian answered the phone, talked briefly with him, couldn't readily address the issue, and handed the phone to me. Why not, I'm the one who wrote the obituary. The conversation went something like this:

Undertaker: "Hello, Judi, how are you holding up?"

Me: "I guess I'm okay. I don't really know."

Undertaker: "Please know we're praying for you and your family and we love you all."

Me: "Thank you, that means a lot. We appreciate it greatly."

Undertaker: "I was telling Brian that we can't put the reason for Jenson's death in his obituary."

Me: "Why not?"

Undertaker: "We just can't put it in that way."

Me: "But why?"

Undertaker: "If we put it in the way you wrote it, it will disturb people. We really need to use words like 'suddenly' or 'unexpectedly.'"

Me: "When you use words like that, people know it's probably a suicide anyway, so why does it matter?"

Undertaker: "If we say someone took their own life, it really bothers and disturbs the people who read it. It makes them really uncomfortable."

Me: "So we're not supposed to tell the truth because it makes people uncomfortable?"

Undertaker: "Well, yes."

Brian then weighs in, his tone very distraught: "Jude, maybe we should just do what he wants us to do if that's what's normal."

Me to Brian, getting even more agitated: "No, I don't care what's normal; I want to tell the truth."

Me to undertaker: "I don't care if people are disturbed by what I wrote; this is about Jenson and our family, not about some reader's comfort level."

Undertaker: "You just can't put it in the paper that way."

Me: "That's the way I want it put in."

Undertaker: "I understand, but we don't write the real reason in regard to a suicide. We don't say he 'took his own life.'"

Me: "I don't care what you do in other obituaries; I want Jenson's put in the paper the way I wrote it. I'm not going to give in on this point." Now I'm actually crying and trying to speak clearly and distinctly. "I want you to put the obituary in the paper exactly the way I wrote it. I'm not leaving out the words 'took his own life.' Please put it in the way I wrote it. I don't care what people think, and I don't care what other people do. I want it this way."

The undertaker finally conceded, but I knew it was against his better judgment. He was the expert on obituaries, but I refused to budge simply because of reader comfort level. Since he cared so much for us, I also assume he was concerned about our personal welfare and what people would think about our family if they knew how Jenson died. But I didn't care about that in the least.

As it turned out, we received numerous encouraging comments and notes of gratitude for our honesty and bravery after that obituary was printed in the paper. Yes, I was indeed determined to be honest, but at that point, being brave was not on my radar and never entered my mind. Brian and I have never once tried to cover up or change the factuality of how Jenson died. Speaking and facing the truth have allowed us a much more thorough healing process. Lysa TerKeurst declares, "Honesty isn't trying to hurt me. It's trying to heal me."[11]

Other than two trips out and Jenson's memorial service, I didn't leave our house for any length of time during the two weeks after December 23rd. However, cleaning up demanded

entrance back into the world, so the day after the service, I got
up and put on mascara and eyeliner, thus marking my entry
back into the land of the living. I needed to learn to live outside
my house again, but how was that supposed to work?

Would people look at me and see Jenson had died by suicide? Was it even worth putting on eye makeup, because it
would just wash off with my tears when I started crying, yet
again? I didn't know, but I had to do something normal, because
everything else felt odd, and strange, and irrational, and
out of balance. Putting on eye makeup was a task I could
accomplish with no thought, so that was what I did.

In the "Heaven Sent" season-nine episode of *Doctor Who*,
the Doctor tells us that the day we lose a loved one isn't the
worst because at least we have something to do that day.
However, he then continues with this thought: "It's all the days
they stay dead."[12]

What would I now do with all the days ahead that Jenson
stayed dead? Cleaning up would only last so long, and then
what? Shock was still calling the shots, so I just did the next
thing and helped Brian with whatever he needed to do in order
to obtain the closure of Jenson's paperwork, a challenge indeed.

It was his finances that had to be cleaned up next. Because
he was eighteen when he died and had no will, this was difficult, a headache we just didn't need so soon after his death.
He was considered to be of legal adult status, so dealing with
his money was an arduous and troubling task that would have
involved far less bureaucracy had he been two months younger
at his time of death.

Bureaucracy offers no pity in loss, not even the loss of a
child. None of the people with whom we dealt extended any
compassion over Jenson's death when our reason for contending
with his paper trail was verbalized by our grieving-parent lips.

Brian wasn't allowed to close out Jenson's college-
investment funds without going to the Surrogate's Court

and creating a new estate so everything could be transferred to that account. This court is in the basement of our local county building—a dark and gloomy place, even on a sunny day. Whose idea was it for people to have to address their dead loved one's paperwork in the worst possible location for someone trudging through the grief of their loss? Our taxes can't pay for something better than a windowless basement for this demoralizing chore?

Brian then took care of the bulk of the rest of Jenson's financial paperwork while I offered to go to the bank and close out his savings account. We decided to empty his passbook by transferring the money into Kalina's account. Later we would give Tyler half of that money, but at the time it was easier just to think about closing all of Jenson's accounts as quickly as possible.

The teller at the bank where he had his savings was insistent on knowing why I was closing the account. "I can't close out this account without a reason," I was told.

I responded, "I just need to close it."

"I understand that, but I need a reason for doing so."

"You can't just please close it at my request?" I replied, with a bit more agitation.

"Ma'am, I need to write down the reason for doing so."

"I don't understand why a reason has anything to do with it. It's my son's savings account, and I just want to close it and transfer the money into my daughter's account."

"The form requires I put down a reason. I need to write something on the line that asks for that," she said in a somewhat more callous tone.

We had a brief visual standoff while my eyes filled with tears and I finally blurted out more loudly than I intended, "Because he's dead, is that reason enough for you?"

Customers at other windows and employees behind the counter were now staring at me. Perhaps, had I put my hand in my pocket at that moment, they would have all fallen to the floor, fearing what I planned to pull out and point at the teller at whom I was glaring so despairingly.

But my teller continued gawking at me and said nothing, as if my words didn't compute in her bureaucratic brain. I was just about ready to plead for the branch manager's help when her mouth finally opened and she uttered something, but never an apology for any of it, not even "I'm so sorry for the loss of your son."

She completed the transaction, and I exited, head down in despondency. Walking to my car where Kalina was waiting, my tears flowed freely as my body sank into the driver's seat.

The last thing I wanted to do was hurt my precious daughter in any way, but I was thinking about my bank experience rather than about upsetting her with my crying. She asked me what happened, and after I told her about the hassle of the money transfer I added that it wasn't right that any of us should profit from Jenson's death because no one should ever benefit when someone else dies.

However, the truth is people benefit from another person's death on a regular basis. There are inheritances, legacies, scholarships, financial gifts, and more. And let's not forget what Jesus did for all of us when He went to the cross so we could spend eternity in Heaven. The reality of Kalina's college years was that there wouldn't be much concern for her financially because half of Jenson's college savings went to fund her education. What a tangled web of blessing and brokenness intertwined together.

Not all of the after-suicide cleaning up of our lives was difficult, especially the portions for which we held no responsibility. The tentacles of Jenson's deadly choice reached far into the local communities and activities of the capital district surrounding us. Due to the widespread knowledge of his death and the large volume of teens who knew him, the regional chapter of an international Christian organization decided to change the topics at their Saratoga Springs City Center youth conference in January of 2012.

Excel, the high school ministry convention of Youth for Christ, chose to forgo their original subject matter and instead address suicide, grief, and how God fits into the picture. This would involve over one thousand teenagers discussing and dealing with a topic that is rarely addressed in Christianity.

Brian and I were glad this difficult theme was being talked about; God knows we hoped it would prevent other parents from living our nightmare. But there was no relief from the fact that the change was due to our own son's choice. What parent would be grateful for that?

There were other fleeting moments of comfort and encouragement that came to us along the path we now walked because of Jenson's decision. However, the benefits to our grieving hearts weren't worth the loss of our precious son. Jerry Sittser, who lost his wife, mother, and only daughter in a single car accident, describes our sentiments with these words in his *A Grace Disguised*: "The good that may come out of the loss does not erase its badness . . ."[13]

We wish it hadn't had to be Jenson's death that precipitated others' contemplation of future choices. Why does it so often have to be a tragedy that causes people to value life in a greater way? One person's loss is often another person's gain, but there is no emotional fairness in the balance of these opposites. Loss and gain are the antithesis of each other, not opportunity equalizers.

Something to Consider: First of all, please make sure your children have a will when they turn eighteen years of age. No one anticipates the death of someone that young, but if it happens, a will has the capability of removing a great weight from your shoulders when your brain is just barely functioning in its grief.

Secondly, please don't remind grieving parents of the possible good things that came out of their child's death. It isn't your job to be the voice that speaks that into someone's life. If you want to share something you specifically learned, be cautious how you phrase it, so it doesn't come across as a really upbeat "But look at how much good came out of this."

I had a student who told me she hadn't wanted to go to Jenson's memorial service because she'd been so demoralized by what had been said at the funeral of another teen who died by his own hand. The pastor at that funeral told everyone suicide was the "unpardonable sin" and the dead teen wouldn't be allowed into Heaven. How can that ever possibly be a correct pastoral choice, no matter what someone believes? That pastor should be defrocked.

My student said she loved Jenson so much and didn't think she could bear to listen to bad things said about him at his service, but since it was such a loving service, she'd been greatly relieved to see a more compassionate side of God. She was thankful she made the choice to attend after all.

She missed Jenson very much and cried while telling me this. There was nothing upbeat or cheerful about her words, and I was thankful she shared this with me. She wasn't trying to remind me of anything good that came out of Jenson's death. She was merely sharing with me about the loss of him in her life and how consoled she was at his service.

CHAPTER 5

"What Is This Feeling?"
(Grief)

Since Jenson was so photogenic and cooperative when he was a youngster, he was hired to be in three commercials before reaching his teen years. One of those was just him alone, and the other two were with Kalina. His TV-advertising career was rather short-lived, though. He liked the idea of getting a paycheck, but that wasn't enough to feed an interest in being on the big screen. Fascinated as he was by film, his preference lay behind a camera rather than in front of one. Jenson knew his own mind and acted accordingly as he grew older.

Shock is an amazing gift, especially when we don't know our own minds. It protects us in the early days of our raw and all-consuming grief. It's what allows us to function through the devastation and tragedy of our circumstances. Our family was able to manage daily life throughout several weeks after Jenson's suicide because of that shock.

However, we desperately needed to find a qualified grief counselor, sooner rather than later. Our pastor and friends had been loving and supportive, but they weren't trained in counseling suicide survivors. A suicide death dumps a huge amount of trauma on a family. The survivors have an especially difficult time absorbing the circumstances of a loved one's choice to take his or her life.

Since it was the Christmas holiday week after Jenson's death, I couldn't get ahold of any professional counselors. Every name or lead given to me was fruitless. I was desperate to find someone who could help our family, especially my three cherished ones I loved so greatly. Their obvious pain magnified my pain, and it was disheartening to continually hit the wall of no help.

Finally, the head of our homeschool co-op called to tell me she'd been able to make an appointment for us to go see someone at a Christian counseling center. She declared he met my one and only criterion by saying he'd dealt with suicide before. I was adamant that we had to see someone who had counseled suicide survivors in the past. So almost a week after Jenson's death, our now four-membered family headed off to see this counselor—our first time leaving the house since suicide hijacked our hearts.

We were so hopeful this counselor could help us in our anguish and distress that there was even a bit of lighthearted banter on the way. Rather than reaching out to us in our complete and total brokenness, though, he was more concerned about doing an insurance intake, which added even greater weight to our despondency. What was he thinking? And why did insurance matter that day, anyway—our homeschool group had gifted us with the payment. He would get his money.

When Brian and I sat down, I asked, "Have you ever counseled a family with a suicide before?"

"I can deal with that," he responded, and then continued filling out the form on his clipboard.

That response was a clue that he didn't know what he was doing. If he'd really counseled suicide survivors, he would've said, "Yes, I have," wouldn't he?

After his inability to answer in the affirmative, we should've gotten up and walked out, but we were shattered, desolate, and confused. Making spontaneous decisions for our own good wasn't much of a consideration in our fragile state of mind.

That counselor was no help, at all. The longer he talked, the more aggravated Brian became as our one allotted hour advanced toward its end, and Tyler and Kalina had not been invited in to join us yet. The counselor left them sitting in the waiting room while he talked to us first; it was Brian who finally insisted they be given time before we had to leave. As it turned out, our precious children received ten minutes of interaction with that counselor and no more. Ten minutes was all he was willing to invest in them less than a week after seeing their brother dead on the floor in front of them.

We desperately needed a lifeline, yet this man seemed to care more about whether insurance would cover our future counseling sessions or not. I wanted to weep. He had the opportunity to be the hands and feet of Jesus to us, and instead, he left us drowning in our grief and confusion; shame on him.

We left that counseling session highly agitated and no better off than before we'd gotten there. Where were we possibly going to find someone who could help us, someone who had spent real time counseling suicide survivors? That answer lay with hospice; who would have guessed? It had never even occurred to me they would have someone who could help in regard to a suicide death, so of course I never contacted them during my initial search.

A few days after Jenson died, one of the homeschool moms in our co-op, a hospice nurse, arranged for a trained suicide counselor to come talk to the teens who knew Jenson. This counselor had dealt with teen suicides in the past and regularly went into public schools to talk with students after such a death. She and the mom knew each other through their shared work.

To our great relief, this same hospice counselor also agreed to meet with us as a family. She was an answer to our prayer and the lifeline we needed for practical help and advice on what to do and how to heal. She gave us concrete, tangible physical and mental exercises to practice so we could endure our initial grief and make it through Jenson's memorial service. I will always credit her counseling with saving us when we needed it most.

It's so very interesting to me that she didn't come from a faith-based practice, and yet she, not the Christian counselor we first visited, is the one who actually upheld and aided us. People who haven't had hands-on experience and training with suicide survivors don't have the needed expertise for such. Yes, survivors need people to pray for them and encourage them, but their grief is so horrifically singular and needs specific counseling intervention.

There's a devastating stigma upon those left behind, bringing greater shame and guilt. We often don't know the reason for the suicide, so there appears to be no one to blame but ourselves. Some people seem more than ready to blame us, too, and they're quite vocal about that—thankfully, though, not typically in close proximity to our ears. We hear about it from others.

Suicide deaths have to be investigated as if a crime has taken place, which leaves even more carnage in its wake with the involvement of the police. Sometimes there's even media coverage proclaiming the news to anyone listening, reading, or watching. The people who respond to survivors after learning about them from the media are not usually the ones from whom you want to hear.

It's frequently a family member who finds the body, leaving that person with PTSD and flashbacks of the death scene. If the suicide happens in the house where the family lives, they're always reminded of that fact as they cohabitate with disturbing memories. Far too consistently, the first words out of someone's mouth when they find out about the suicide are "How did he/she do it?" We love gruesome details, don't we! We listen to those details and then feel compelled to pass them on, sometimes even in the form of a prayer request. How sad.

In addition to continuing to see the hospice counselor regularly, I also began seeing someone on my own. My dear friend Kate sent me to her, and she was another lifeline who had also dealt with suicide before.

Still reeling from the experience with the male counselor we'd originally seen, after sitting down with this new woman I asked, "I know you need my insurance information; would you like that now before we begin?"

She simply stated, "We'll talk about that another time, but not today. Tell me about Jenson." And I cried because I felt like I'd found another home for my grief.

Even now, all this time since Jenson's death, I still occasionally go see this same woman when I sense the need. There's no shame in ever asking for help with our mental and emotional needs. Those needs are equally important to anything we may require physically.

This counselor is a woman of faith but not in a faith-based practice. How could the two women we were seeing, not part of any Christian counseling center, be so much more loving, kind, useful, and accommodating than one who claims the name of Jesus on a sign outside his front door? It made no sense to me, but I was grateful we hadn't given up after our first disheartening experience. Not everyone who claims the name of Jesus is truly His hands and feet or has answers for those desperately staring down a crisis.

It was by the grace of God, the help of our counselors, and the love of various dear people that I was able to wade through the first several months after Jenson died. I had many commitments consuming my brain space, which may well have been the reason I was able to function as well as people thought I was. However, there came a point when those commitments waned, and I had more time on my hands. I'm not suggesting that people should stay really busy while grieving, but the busyness did help me survive for about five months as I fulfilled commitments I felt required to by my journey.

Our hospice counselor told us people have to grieve at some point. If they don't do it sooner, they do it later. We can run from grief, but it eventually catches up with us, even if it's many years down the road. Also, if we grieve later rather than sooner, it's often more difficult to wade through the muck of it all. Even though I thought I was dealing well with my grief, my muck got really deep before I was able to pull my feet out of the suction of the ache pulling me down into a ruptured relationship with the God I had followed since my teen years—but more on that to come.

Although I felt like I was sinking, I still wrote the following in my journal: "I don't mind the pain. I want to go as far into it as I need to so I can heal all the way to the depth of my wounded brokenness." I just somehow knew if I was going to live through the grief, I was going to have to go as deep into my emotional and spiritual darkness as needed to get to the light on the other side of that horrible pain.

And I would have to learn to hold on to that light, once I could keep it in my sight line, because the pain didn't just subside following a few months of struggling. Even after some years' time I would write, "Sometimes the grief and the sorrow and the missing of Jenson are so strong, so palpable, I feel swallowed up by them, as if I have fallen into a dark place from which I can never leave . . . I hate feeling that way, so lost, so dark, so completely alone."

As years progressed that darkness came less frequently, but even now, sometimes it rears its ugly head, and I'm thankful I fought the fight and learned the skills necessary to survive. Jerry Sittser admonishes, "The quickest way to reach the light of day is to head east, plunge into darkness until one comes to the sunrise."[14] I will always be grateful for the grace that granted me the instinct to run headlong into the pain, not away from it. We must claim that grace for our body, soul, and mind in order to do the intense labor involved in healing that grief requires of us.

In his book *Understanding Your Suicide Grief*, Alan D. Wolfelt tells us grief and mourning are not the same things. He defines grief as "the compilation of thoughts and feelings that welled up within you when you first encountered this painful loss and that remain inside you as you cope with changes that this loss has brought in your life."[15] However, he goes on to say that mourning is actively and purposefully moving grief from the inside to the outside and expressing it externally.

I want to be known as a woman who has both grieved and mourned well, for without both, there can be no rescue and recovery from the abyss of despair. And the ache of grief does indeed feel like an abyss at times, but I'm here to tell you there is a goodly measure of deliverance when grief is owned, faced, and turned into active, healthy mourning.

I've worked hard to impel my grief from the inside to the outside, and I will most likely have to keep working at it for the rest of my life, for grief, as it progresses, is like the ever changeable weather, where one day it's dark and rainy and the very next moment the sky can open up clear and beautiful. In the reality of my grief and mourning, I acknowledged every bit of both the dark and rainy emotions as well as the clear and beautiful ones, no matter how, when, or where those opposites affected me. And I need to tell you . . . they still do affect me, just not in extremes the way they once did.

In my journal I wrote, "I want to wrap my heart, mind, soul, and faith around every feeling, tear, pain, and all else during this journey. I don't want to miss or pass over anything so as to make it [the journey] go faster." I believe the grace that allowed me to wrestle with the truth, whatever it appeared to be at any given moment after Jenson's suicide, is the same grace that has also transformed me throughout this journey of "daze" since his death.

I do, however, understand why some people walk away from a loved one's suicide without ever looking back at that event again. It must appear easier to deal with reality that way. Transformation and change can be really difficult and uncomfortable. But walking away and pretending a suicide didn't happen doesn't allow us to take control of our grief and pain on our own terms. C. S. Lewis declares, "There is nothing we can do with suffering except to suffer it."[16] Grief demands we have to suffer. Healing demands we have to own that suffering.

There comes a point when the only way through and forward in our healing is to stop thinking and living like a victim and become a survivor instead. I'm not saying it's wrong to be a victim. We can't be a survivor if we were never a victim in the first place. Continuous victim mentality, however, doesn't trudge through the hard and demanding work of healing.

The father of Columbine's Rachel Scott speaks this to us out of his own grief journey: "You have to learn to see [move] through the event and not get stuck in it."[17] Forever remaining a victim is passive, whereas becoming a survivor is active and progressive. If we're going to persist and endure, we have to own the work involved in surviving beyond the trauma or tragedy that made us a victim in the first place. We do need initial victim time so healing can begin with the acceptance of our loss, but it's essential we venture on to becoming a survivor in order to live in and through the redemption that can lead us out of our miserable circumstances.

Perhaps, for some it seems safer to remain a victim and not move forward to experiencing the regeneration and redefinition that grace the life of a survivor. If we remain victims for too long, though, we reconceive what normal feels like and choose to stay where grief found us and then left us. By not working to climb out of the pit of despair, we may just stay there for the rest of our days—almost like a second death after the one that sent us to that pit in the first place.

Life is ever moving, and as we move with it our grief becomes a permanent accessory in the backpacks of our brokenness. There is always pain that accompanies it and a constant ache of tentacle-reminders around our hearts. Jerry Sittser says, "Pain will have its way because loss is undeniably, devastatingly real."[18] I think it's what we do with loss and grief that defines us either as continual victims or as those who actively participate in our survival.

We can run from grief, but we can never escape it, nor can we ignore it, try as we may. Grief will always catch up with us eventually, and if we don't stand face to face with it and admit the truth about our brokenness, we can't heal. And if we don't face it sooner rather than later, it will be worse later and leave even more carnage in its wake. We have to deal with grief, or it will deal with us in ways that are unhealthy, ways that take their toll on our well-being and the well-being of those whom we love.

Much of life is made up of continual intimations of our loss. Specific dates fill us with anticipated apprehension and maudlin memories every time they show up on a calendar. Grief is allowed no passivity on these days. Jenson's death on the twenty-third day of a month brought that reminder on every twenty-third of every month for years on end. Tyler's birthday is also on a twenty-third of a month, bringing even more grief because of what that date now meant to his precious life.

I don't remember when every single twenty-third actually stopped calling out for recognition. Sometimes, even now, a happening on a twenty-third of no particular month makes me take notice, and I remember how long it took me to stop holding my breath from a twenty-second to a twenty-fourth before every flip of a calendar page. The cognizance of no longer holding my breath brought relief for finally forgetting, but guilt followed, too, for the same reason. This is the nature of grief.

In my journal, I wrote I wanted the journey of grief to be my home as long as I needed it to be for the sake of my personal healing. This was in response to Steve Green's song "I Will Go," in which he sings of choosing to go wherever the road leads, while praying for strength, regardless of the difficulties because his life belongs to God.[19]

This song has a very different interpretation in my head and heart than it did for the years of singing it before Jenson's suicide. As a matter of fact, much of my life is now viewed through a different lens, one so very dissimilar to the time before I lost a child to death. Grief has caused me to value life in a greater way, but also to admit how fleeting our treasured moments can be and, therefore, to not cling to anything but Jesus too tightly.

Something to Consider: It's not your job to try to pull someone out of their "victim" moments of grief. Everyone grieves so very differently, and no one needs to be told they ought to be done with it, or be judged if they seem to no longer be demonstrating their loss the way you think they should. How someone grieves and mourns will change from day to day.

So much of personal grief is directly related to personality, faith, background, family baggage, education, coping mechanisms, present circumstances, and more. Ways and longevity of grieving are as different as hair colors, body types, and shoe sizes; there is no one-size-fits-all. Give the grace you would wish to receive if roles were reversed.

For some, grief and mourning will both take much longer than you think. For others, they may be briefer but also catch the grieving person unawares when least expected. Grief and mourning don't stop; they just change costumes for the next scene in the production of life that never ends until the curtain closes with our final breath.

CHAPTER 6

"To Life"
(Fiddler on the Roof)

Jenson's theatrical tour de force was playing the part of Tevye, at age sixteen, in the teen production of *Fiddler on the Roof* I was directing. At auditions, I only had two choices of young men I believed could pull off that part. Since I tried to avoid nepotism casting, at all costs, I always had other adults—my producer, my choreographer, my accompanist and her husband, and one or two others—on my audition committee so they could give their input, too. I trusted these people, and they knew they could be honest about decisions if they didn't agree with me. Casting time was a safe and congenial place for all of us to speak our minds.

Even though Jenson had only done comedic roles—in *Anne of Green Gables* at age twelve and in *Snoopy!!!: The Musical*, as Pigpen, at age fourteen—I knew he could play Tevye. However, casting the other young man in that lead role and giving Jenson a different part was also an option. I left the decision up to my committee; they chose Jenson.

Although hesitant in his own ability to take on such a broad and immense character, he really did want the part. His huge smile at the offer of Tevye gave that away. Thus began the task of building his confidence and getting him to believe he could pull off the lead.

He started voice lessons to boost his singing. He was good friends with the young woman who would play his wife, a tremendous plus for reassuring the ease of that relationship. He was extremely fond of the teen girls playing his daughters. His best friend was also in the show, as were Kalina and several other people to whom he was close. These offstage relationships helped with his comfort level and made rehearsals a safe place to work on developing who both he and I thought Tevye should be.

About a month before our own *Fiddler* was to open, we attended another local high school production of that show. I wanted to see what it was like, and we were borrowing several of their set pieces after the final performance. Jenson didn't care much for their Tevye. Although he wasn't extremely critical, I could tell he was processing what he saw that actor do onstage.

After that night, my noncompetitive son became a much larger, funnier, louder, and more commanding Tevye during rehearsals. Taking him to see that performance was the best thing I could have done to get him to own his character. Who would have guessed that?

There were specific rehearsal moments that bolstered Jenson's confidence, too. He'd been working with the choreographer on "If I Were a Rich Man," but I hadn't seen the number, not even at home when he was practicing the lyrics and dance steps. The day came for him to do the song in front of the whole cast.

As we watched him gesticulate, shake his hips, snap his fingers, and move his feet around every inch of the stage, all of us, teens and production staff alike, laughed our way through the entire piece. There was on-and-off applause and rousing cheers while he performed, rising to an out-of-control crescendo when he was done. Dropping his final pose, he looked around the room and his face lit up, not as Tevye but as Jenson no longer doubting himself or his ability to portray that character.

Closer to opening night, we were working on the scene where Tevye's middle daughter, Chava, has come to speak with him after her secret marriage to a Russian soldier. Tevye is devastated by her betrayal and cannot willingly accept her and her new husband. This scene is an amazingly troubling and aching moment in the show—the daughters dance together in dreamlike fashion as Tevye argues with himself about all he believes. The audience needs to feel the heart-wrenching turmoil and ache that is often the very real and difficult stuff of parenting.

The scene was going okay, but not to the depth I desired. I couldn't seem to make Jenson understand the actual pain Tevye would feel. Why should he? He was only sixteen and had never been a father. I don't even remember what I said or exactly how I demonstrated what I wanted, but I moved Jenson out of the way and began improvising the emotion I expected from Tevye as I acted out the part myself. Jenson watched and said nothing. Then I moved offstage and told everyone we were doing the scene again.

At the end, when Tevye declares he "cannot bend that far or he will break," picks up his cart, and walks away from Chava, there was dead silence in the rehearsal room. My face was wet with tears, and as I slowly turned my head to look at the others, I could see glistening wetness on several cheeks. One of the teen boys began slowly and methodically clapping as others moved their hands and joined in. Applause circled the room as we exhaled our emotions and dried our eyes on our sleeves. Jenson and I and everyone in that space knew he'd nailed it.

Tevye was Jenson's from that point on, and other than giving a few specific stage movements, I didn't have to explain much of anything to him after that. The innate sensitivity he possessed, along with his understanding nature, gave him the ability to breathe life into his character onstage. And after the Schenectady Light Opera Company's high school musical competition committee came to see the show, he received a nomination for Outstanding Actor for his portrayal of Tevye, even though he didn't ultimately win that award.

Schenectady Light Opera Company was actually mounting its own production of *Fiddler on the Roof* at the end of March 2012, after Jenson's death. The director had emailed me in early December asking me to audition for the character of either Golde or Fruma-Sarah. Although honored to be asked, I didn't give much thought to participating since I figured I'd be too busy directing *Seussical.* Then, with Jenson's suicide, any thought about SLOC's *Fiddler* left my brain along with every bit of normal daily thinking. In other words, there was no room for contemplating auditioning, so I completely forgot; the only thoughts filling my brain after 12/23/2011 were about Jenson and the rest of my immediate family.

However, a few days before Jenson's memorial service, the director contacted me again and asked me to come down to callbacks and sing for the part of Fruma-Sarah. She knew about Jenson's suicide and told me I could show up to sing when no one was there so I didn't have to see people or be part of a crowd. Apparently she knew, as well as I did, I couldn't handle a crowd less than two weeks after losing Jenson. I didn't honestly know if I could manage just the director and the accompanist, let alone sing anything for an audition.

In reality, I had my doubts I could even maneuver being in *Fiddler*, at all, period. All the scenes of Jenson's Tevye played through my mind like a movie. How could I stand to watch someone else do that part? How could my family and friends watch the entire musical less than two years since Jenson had the lead? How could I sing, act, move, or any of it, onstage with all those achingly beautiful Jenson-as-Tevye memories pulsing through my brain above my hurting heart? I stared and thought, and stared and thought, and finally asked Brian what I should do, but he didn't know, either. After our child's suicide, how do any of us know what will be good for us and what won't?

Making a last-minute decision to go sing, I entered the theater and sat down to wait, hoping to see no one but the two I expected to be there. The director came in, sat next to me, and said, "I'm so sorry about your son's suicide. My sister took her life a few years ago."

I think I said something in response, but who knows what that was.

"It's a horrible thing to live through for those who are left behind," she continued. "I want you to know I'm a woman of faith, too, and I'm praying for you. I won't be able to come to your son's memorial service, though, because I'll be away this weekend. Do you think you can sing for us now?"

This was my first introduction to the unsought learning about the prevalence of suicide in society. Now that it was part of my own story, I would far too often hear how many other families were affected by it, too. I don't mind knowing, though. When you feel as if you are the only person walking a suicide road, it really does bring some sort of odd comfort to know you share a similar story with someone else.

The day after that quasi-audition the director called and offered me the part of Fruma-Sarah. She wanted me to be in her production as part of my "healing process." Up to that point, no one had used those words with me. I couldn't say no but wondered how my choice of "yes" would play out into something possibly resembling "healing."

As time progressed, it became clear to me it was indeed a good choice. The cast of SLOC's *Fiddler*, many whom knew me well and attended Jenson's memorial service, was extremely kind, loving, and supportive throughout our months of rehearsals and the performances. It was good for me to be in a safe place, with calm and comfortable people, who weren't personally grieving the loss of my son and therefore not draining me the way so many others in my life were doing in the aftermath of his suicide.

It was amusing to me how I had frequently joked, during Jenson's *Fiddler*, that I wanted to be Fruma-Sarah because it's such a fun character role. I would go over-the-top in demonstrating what I desired from my own Fruma-Sarah when I was giving her directions. Now it was my opportunity to go over-the-top for real. Here I was playing that part, without Jenson and the other teens, without seeking it out, and without any kind of normal audition. In hindsight, what a hoot!

Plus, with the director's desire for something different from normal for my character, I was performing on Rollerblades. I skated through the theater, up a ramp, around the stage a few times, and out the side curtain all while singing at the top of my lungs. Fruma-Sarah is not a nice person, so letting her rip was an emotional release for me. The Rollerblades added to the fun and laughter, and indeed, it was healing.

Something to Consider: Please use caution when suggesting to someone that what they're doing in their grief journey may not be the right decision. I'm fully aware counselors tell you not to make major life changes—a new job, a new house, moving cross-country, giving away your pet, et cetera—the first year after someone you love dies. However, something that might be a burden for one person, like being in a musical, might be a burden-lifter for another. There should be a great deal of freedom for people to grieve in a way that actually allows them some healing. Give a grieving person the grace to seek healthy activities that bring them joy. It's hard to find joy in the first year or two after losing someone you love.

CHAPTER 7

"Get Me to the Church on Time" (No, Please Don't—Church)

As a child, Jenson wasn't competitive or aggressive. He wasn't much interested in team sports or large-group activities. Although he willingly took part in activities like swim team and soccer, he didn't apply himself and would spend his time socializing with just one or two people he liked. To the dismay of his other teammates, the ball frequently rolled right past his feet while he was chitchatting with a friend on the soccer field. It's a good thing we were never a big team- or individual-sports family. That lifestyle would have been miserable for my younger son.

He did like activities like bike riding, roller skating, swimming (for fun only), and outdoor games with small groups of friends or his family. Had I been more observant of Jenson in his younger years I might have noticed his introverted proclivity toward very small numbers for his socializing choices. However, at that time, I still had no idea there was a distinct difference between being antisocial and being an introvert.

Heaven forbid any of my homeschooled three should ever be described as antisocial; perish the thought.

As Jenson moved toward his eighteen-year-old self, he began sharing articles with me about introverts. Aha . . . those articles explained a lot. Wish I'd read them when he was younger; he was indeed an introvert. Although he very much liked his time with friends, his creative juices flowed when he was alone, not in a large-group setting where everyone was talking at the same time.

Because of Jenson, I learned I'm an introvert, too. No wonder I hate chaos. No wonder I always wanted my children's friends to go home after two hours at my house. No wonder three-or-more-hour musical rehearsals with a large number of teens drained my social limits. No wonder too much talk around me depletes the creativity I have when I'm alone. No wonder church has been a somewhat difficult place to be since Jenson died. Church is not typically a healthy, nurturing place for introverts, especially introverts who are grieving.

After Jenson's suicide, we didn't start attending church regularly until later in January. The only reason we went at that time was due to feeling pressured by our pastor to come back. I think he thought it would help us to see how much people loved us, and of course, as a pastor, where else do you want your congregation to be on a Sunday morning?

My guess is pastors think their church is a healing place and the body of Christ is the most loving group there is for someone in the throes of grief and loss. However, this wasn't true for us, and although we were greatly loved as we did our slow walk through the valley of the shadow of death, much of our wounding was effectuated by those within the church and the body of Christ at large—not purposefully, but out of ignorance. But even when things are done out of ignorance rather than purposefully, the end result is most often just as detrimental.

Our first trip back to church was overwhelming. Between the distress of a dear friend who accompanied us and the volume of people trying so hard to show us they loved us, we would have felt less anxiety had we waited a few more Sundays before attending again. Brian was especially uncomfortable and appeared near an emotional breakdown as people approached. Thankfully, our pastor had the good sense to try to steer several congregants away from us. I know everyone meant well, but we realized just how much we didn't want to talk to people until we were ready, and we most certainly weren't ready on that Sunday just two weeks after Jenson's memorial service.

Even after that, attending church on a regular basis and experiencing the emotional roller coaster of listening to the music and the messages and being confronted by so many people continued to be taxing. Tears were often my deepest form of worship for weeks of Sunday mornings. People tried to be gentle and kind, but it didn't help. I so often felt drained and psychologically spent inside God's house, as if I were being depleted by comforting others who were clueless as to how to comfort me.

At the end of a service, only a couple of weeks after we'd begun attending again, our pastor's wife walked up to me with her arm around a weeping, distraught woman. This woman was so upset by Jenson's suicide that she was on the verge of hysterics by the time she opened her mouth to speak to me. She sobbed out her apology for not attending his memorial service because of her own devastation over his death. As she grabbed me and clung to my body in her anguish, I could feel a sense of panic rising from her constriction of my movement. I needed her to leave my emotional space as soon as possible, so I immediately blurted out, "It's okay you didn't go to Jenson's service. You don't need to apologize or say anything else. I understand."

Our pastor's wife thanked me for comforting this woman, but as they walked back down the aisle I thought, "Dear God, I'm the one whose son is dead; what are these people thinking by burdening me this way?" They weren't thinking, though, at least not about my personal distress, and that was why things like this happened on a fairly regular basis. It was such a hardship to carry the grief of others while I was consumed with my own pain.

None of these people seemed able to put themselves in my shoes because none of them had dealt with a suicide before. Our church had never dealt with a suicide before. There was no manual, and no one knew what to do, so we were at the mercy of the bereavement whims of the body of Christ and the church at large. It was exhausting at times.

During the spring and summer of that first year of Jenson's death, Brian met fairly regularly with our pastor for what might be labeled as "counseling" sessions. I was asked to join them at some point in July or August when I was home from the Adirondacks. My pastor wanted to connect with me to see how I was doing. I'm seldom in my home church during the summer months, and he hadn't seen me for a few weeks.

Of course our discussion was about Jenson, and at one point I must have looked sad, because I was told to "SMILE!!!" The command was spoken somewhat kindly, but I was appalled at his demand. I could see Brian's fists tighten in dismay and wondered, "Is he going to punch the man?" Why would someone in a pastoral position think it was appropriate to tell me to smile when we were talking about my dead son who'd been gone less than eight months? Wasn't it enough I wasn't crying like I still did on a regular basis?

Although he'd been absolutely wonderful in the early days after Jenson died, it became very clear to me that our pastor now had no clue as to the depth of our brokenness and lingering pain. He was no longer safe for my grieving heart, so I never spoke of my bereavement to him again after that meeting. He had lost his credibility to speak into my life.

Had our pastor falsely believed that looking and acting like everything was fine was the way to recover? He had espoused "fake it till you make it" to Brian several times during their counseling sessions, which always disturbed me. Did he really believe that? Was he part of the church culture that believes we should all look and act "happy" no matter what happens in our lives, that glaring lie perpetuated by the "health and wealth gospel"? "We who follow Jesus need not hide our hurts. Not all wounds need covering"[20]; thank you, William Ritter.

Although this man ceased to be a support for me, I did rest in the shelter of those in our Adirondack chapel that summer after Jenson's death. Our mountain congregation is much less uptight and squeaky-clean compared to our Schenectady church. It's not an upper-middle-class body made up of several well-off professionals. It's a fellowship of broken people trying to live and survive in the small-town, impoverished Adirondacks, no easy task. It was much less complicated to be open and honest about my grief with the people at our seasonal church.

I attended their women's Bible study while at our cabin during July and August of 2012, and those dear ladies made me feel loved and accepted no matter what I said. I could speak my heart and mind without being corrected on my theology or chastised for my heavy grief. It was a safe place for me in the midst of my mountain months after Jenson's death. I was extended much grace, and no one told me to "smile!!!"

Something to Consider: Before His time to go to the cross, Jesus told His disciples, "Now is your time of grief, but I will see you again and you will rejoice and no one will take away your joy" (John 16:22). Jesus acknowledges grief and doesn't tell anyone to be or look happy anyway. Nor does He dump His own grief on them. He's masterful at emotional balance and substantiates the spectrum of our feelings.

If we are to be more like Jesus we should neither dump our personal grief on those who are already grieving nor expect the grievers to be upbeat and bubbly if they aren't. Those who are grieving should not have to carry the weight of either of these extremes.

When you're sharing in the grief of someone's particular personal loss, please don't make their loss about you and your needs. Your grief over their loss might actually be a burden to them, but they may not know how to articulate that. When someone is carrying their own grief, or that of their family members, don't dump yours on them, too. It's a weight that shouldn't be added to theirs.

Grace calls for us to lift each other up, not fervently unburden ourselves on someone who is already carrying an excessive amount of their own pain.

CHAPTER 8

"Dogs in the Yard"
(Expectations of Others)

Jenson was an absolutely beautiful child, with gorgeous curly blond hair, straight teeth, and long eyelashes. People often stopped me out in public to comment on his adorableness quotient, sometimes even mistaking him for a little girl when he was a toddler, because he was so darn cute. A year after his death, a stranger would see his senior picture in my wallet and enthusiastically comment on how handsome he was. My tongue refused to tell her he was dead.

I share this to demonstrate that things are not always what they seem to be at first glance. A little boy may be mistaken for a little girl, or vice versa. When a picture of a teenager is viewed, it doesn't occur to the viewer that teen may be dead. Young people aren't supposed to die; you die when you're old. We all think we know more than we likely do and then act according to what we think it is we know, especially in regard to those with whom we share life.

We sometimes place heavy loads on each other without even knowing we're doing it. We frequently assume far too much about ourselves, so we routinely do the same thing with others, too. Some habitually expect too much. These are the folks who usually don't give enough thought as to how their personal activities will affect someone else. They're not particularly adept at putting themselves in the shoes of another person. If they would agree to something, wouldn't everyone?

These people remain unaware when their expectations are a burden rather than a blessing, especially when they have every possible well-meaning intention from the get-go. Every group, family, and organization has them. We can't avoid them, but they can be unnerving and injurious when combined with overwhelming grief. None of us should hold on to our expectations too tightly, because sometimes they suck the life out of the people we love so dearly.

Our niece planned on getting married in Atlanta the day before Easter of 2012, and, of course, we were invited to the wedding. I love my niece; she's a delight. Normally, I would probably say, "Sure, let's go," but since I was in the pangs of a broken heart, I didn't want to attend. However, Brian wouldn't go without me; I continued to be much of his lifeline at that time. And since I was very concerned his sister, our niece's mother, wouldn't be gracious about her brother missing the wedding, I succumbed and went for the sake of the man I loved.

In hindsight, it would have been far better if I'd stuck to my guns and stayed home, even at the risk of offense. It was a really bad choice for me to go. I was an internal mess, and spending time at a large, Southern, extended-family wedding less than four months out from Jenson's suicide was a recipe for emotional disaster. Having to smile, and chitchat, and answer "How are you?" and listen to the delight of others, and try not to be sad, and everything else that goes hand in hand with the excitement of a rehearsal dinner, a wedding, and too many people staying in one house was overwhelmingly difficult.

Personal pain escalated as I watched the happiness on everyone's faces during the wedding ceremony but felt my own heart devoid of joy. Afraid I was going to lose all my suppressed angst at the "for better or for worse" part without ever making it to the "may I present Mr. & Mrs." finality, I sat even more determinedly on my grief so as to allow it no room to creep from hidden crevices.

I was desperately trying to get my mind off my own sorrow; I didn't want to be so distraught on a day that was supposed to be my niece's happiest moment. I didn't want my face to betray my internal struggle, and it took every ounce of self-control to not get up and bolt into the escape of the trees surrounding that outdoor service.

A meltdown finally claimed victory over me as the bride and groom radiantly walked out past rows of rejoicing attendees while I contemplated marriage vows and how anyone could possibly even know what the "for worse" might be while standing at the altar all dewy-eyed with excitement and anticipation over a future spent together. When my emotional dam broke, my mouth uttered words to Brian best left unsaid. By the end of the night, he would be drunk due to magnified grief over my upsetting remarks, not my intention at all.

I spent much of my time alone at the subsequent wedding reception. With everyone laughing, joking, and talking to each other, I felt like a resident alien from a foreign country of heartbreak rather than a partygoer. Tyler and Kalina were off with their cousins, and Brian was drinking and playing cards with his sister's ex-husband, the father of the bride. One of their friends was meandering through the crowd videotaping people as he encouraged everyone to speak wedding wishes to my niece and her new husband.

That gentleman came up and put the camera in my face. "Say something to the newlyweds."

Blocking the filming lens with my hand, I turned away and said with a half smile, "No, thank you. I don't want to say anything or be on video." Words of congratulation were buried deep beneath my busted heart and just wouldn't come out of my mouth at that moment.

But that man wouldn't leave me alone and pushed the camera past my hand even closer to my face. "Oh, come on; say something."

I finally uttered trite words for him to film so he would go away before I lost my composure.

When I stopped speaking into the lens, he turned off the camera and said, "Oh yeah, sorry about your loss," as he moved to the next person and left me staring after him in disbelief.

He knew about Jenson's death and still harassed me into saying something. He knew about Jenson's death and didn't leave me alone when I first said, "No, thank you." He knew about Jenson's death and didn't have enough common sense or tenderness to talk to me like the grieving mother I was. Shame on him, a man who claims to know Jesus and should've known better.

It was demoralizing and heart-wrenching to be in Atlanta for that wedding. It was fine that we'd been invited, but the invitation should have included some sort of comment of understanding about our grief, that if it was easier for us not to come it was okay. Not once, though, were we told to do what was best for us, and if that meant missing this special family event, it was acceptable.

The expectation for us to be at the wedding demonstrated that even when extended family members are sorry for your loss, they don't truly and deeply comprehend the personal pain of losing a child to suicide. I think family believes their grieving loved ones will receive comfort by being with them, but that just isn't true on a regular basis. So often, family is not the compassionate group they perceive themselves to be. Sometimes, extended relatives are just really, really hard in the midst of grief, no matter which side of the family tree spawned them.

My own sister gave me a hard time about our not being home for Christmas of December 2012, a year after Jenson's suicide. Brian was taking us to Grand Cayman, and she let me know she was upset about our going away because she wanted our families to be together instead. I was so disappointed that she didn't seem to understand our need to "get out of Dodge" for the last week of that month of dreadful memories. This was yet another example of people not being supportive of us grieving the way we chose or needed to.

So much of our grief seemed to be fashioned around what other people wanted. If only my sister had given her enthusiastic and encouraging blessing for our time away; she's usually supportive of me, as is Brian's sister with him. Maybe some think they'll be more comforting than they truly will be at specific times. But we are reminded by Jerry Sittser that "Catastrophic loss leaves the landscape of one's life forever changed."[21] Because of that fact, we were desperate to not be home at the difficult time of Jenson's first death anniversary and Christmas of that year, no matter who wanted us to be with them.

Relationship doesn't guarantee a peaceful passage through an extraordinarily painful date. Sometimes the only way to survive is by distance, not proximity, which has nothing to do with any one particular person but merely the location of the brokenhearted griever. There are moments when it doesn't matter whom I'm with; I just don't want to be in a particular place or at a particular gathering, period, and that's all there is to it.

There'll never be a wedding for Jenson, and yet we'll be expected to go to the weddings and bridal showers of friends' and extended family's children. There'll never be grandchildren from Jenson, but we'll be told about all the grandchild escapades of friends' and family's progeny. We'll be included in landmarks that involve the children of extended family and friends, and yet we'll never be able to celebrate any of those same milestones for our Jenson.

My heart desires that someone, somewhere, at these precarious-for-us celebrations, has the compassion to say, "Thank you, so much, for being here. I know how difficult this must be for you, and that makes me even more grateful you would choose to come." Our loss isn't considered in the happiness of others, but I'm also not sure it should be. I honestly don't think I'm coming from a place of jealousy or animosity; I'm just stating the reality of no longer having Jenson events in our future. Kelly Farley and David DiCola describe it this way: "CHEATED . . . I feel cheated out of all the things I would do with my son . . . But most of all, I feel cheated for him, because he will not be able to do them."[22]

So we'll either choose to join friends and family in their celebrations, or we won't go because it's easier for us. Sometimes I can go to things, and sometimes there's just nothing in me that desires to partake in a particular happiness of others, so I stay home. I see this as basic and continual survival, and I no longer blame myself for missing events that call for selfless support.

When one person's happiness overshadows all else, another's pain is imperceptible. I think this is the way most people are wired, especially in a society where being "happy" is often more important than anything else. I'm not blaming anyone for including us in festive and fun life events; I just wish someone, somewhere, would perceive how difficult those may be for us and actually acknowledge that possibility. That would demonstrate astounding discernment.

One of the more difficult expectations catching me completely off guard was that it seemed we should have recovered by the end of the first year after Jenson's death. When we attended church the Sunday after arriving back from Grand Cayman, people actually teased Brian about having pneumonia on our trip (he spent most of his time in the hospital). There were jokes about him wanting extra attention, or that he had to be in the limelight, or other surprisingly flippant comments. No one said, "I'm so very sorry you were sick at such a difficult time for your family."

That was when it appeared that compassion for our grief had pretty much ended now that we'd lived through a full year of no Jenson. I guess we were allotted 365 days, and those days were done. No one seems to speak precise words that give away their thoughts about such, but I sensed a definite shift in behavior from many who knew us. Their actions demonstrated that our grief grace period was over. What those who've not suffered the loss of a child don't seem to comprehend, though, is the truth of Jerry Sittser's words: "Sorrow never entirely leaves the soul of those who have suffered a severe loss."[23]

Since by that second year we were supposed to be "better," "over it," or "back to normal," much of the support and encouragement ended according to people's misconceptions about the length and intensity of grief. Many now stopped talking about Jenson, and there were fewer and fewer posts on his Facebook wall.

However, the second year was more emotionally difficult for me than the first year. I'd held my breath and treaded water for the previous twelve months, hoping I wouldn't drown in grief and sorrow as I counted down through 365 days of survival. Now I faced that second year with the reality of Jenson never returning hitting my brain like the inhale of icy air in subzero temperatures. And even though I'd read that after a death the second year may well be harder than the first, I wasn't prepared for how challenging it would truly be.

I'd thought the first year after Jenson's suicide, that beginning of living through every holiday and function without him, would be the hardest to survive. But it was actually the second year that changed me the most and brought my grief to a higher level of pain and anguish. That first year was a year to concentrate on getting through each day without our son, but the second year was a burning reminder that there would never, ever be a time our Jenson would be a flesh-and-bone part of us again. The first year was about living through continuity, but the second year blazed the reality of our loss into the permanence of our future.

After shouldering up to endure all the firsts of a life without our middle child, my guard was down when the actuality of his special dates were upon us again, and he was still missing, nor would he ever be with us in all our days left on earth. Admitting that truth felt like a tree falling across my chest, suffocating my breath, but I mostly kept this to myself. Whereas the first year had been defined by survival, that second year would be defined by the stark reality of acceptance.

As in any pain, most people don't want to see or know how much the hearts of others suffer, especially when recovery is the greatest goal. We're more comfortable living with the expectation that others are getting "better" and won't be a lifelong drain on our personal contentment or pleasure. We grow weary of listening to the brokenness of those whom we don't see making the progress we think they should be making. But our lack of patience is a gift neither to ourselves nor to the ones we think seem stuck in their loss.

In a culture of "happiness above all else," it's easy to overlook how many of those who are walking their daily lives don't live in happiness, and, therefore, need a huge amount of grace from those who are, or at least pretend they are. Actually, though, we all need grace for as long as we all need grace, which is sort of forever. But Jesus seems to be the only one capable of giving it endlessly, patiently, and lovingly for as long as necessary. The expectations of most of us are not geared toward endless selflessness and longevity. Thank Heaven for Jesus.

Something to Consider: When planning any kind of activity—a wedding, a shower (baby or bridal), a party, a birthday, a religious event, and more—try to expand your thoughts to ponder the circumstances of those you personally know whom you've invited. If you're aware of someone's personal pain, graciously offer your compassion and kindness by saying, "I'd love for you to be a part of this, but I'm also aware it might just be too difficult for you. Therefore, if you'd rather not come, I totally understand. Please do whatever's best for you. Come if you want. Stay home if you want. Leave early if it's too hard to be with all of us. Whatever's best for you! I know you'll be happy for us even if it's too hard for you to join us."

Grace asks us to consider the feelings of others above our own. Please don't allow your personal happiness to overshadow the heart-pain of others. Jesus wasn't a party animal, but even if He had been, I still think He would have looked through the crowd to see who might be having difficulty sharing in His fun. Then He would have put His own pleasure momentarily aside, zeroed in on that person, walked right up to them, and said, "Thank you for sharing in this with me, even though I know your own heart is broken." Jesus always knows whose heart is broken, so maybe He would've also added, "And let me heal that heart for you. That's what I do." That's grace, and mercy, and love . . . putting others before our own pleasure when needed.

CHAPTER 9

"Moments in the Woods" (Parenting)

As Jenson left toddlerhood and moved into his preschool years, he became stubborn, difficult, and temperamental, a regular little pain in the rear end a bit too often. In spite of his affectionate ways, there were times we thought we were raising the Antichrist due to his strong will and tendency toward challenging behavior. He was sent to his room for being rude and ornery at his four-year-old birthday party. While he pouted on his bed, all the other boys and girls partied without him until their parents picked them up.

It was immediately after that party that he decided he no longer wanted to live with us, which was vocalized in a very clear and distinct manner. He was adamant about moving out, so I made arrangements for him to go live with one of his friends who'd been at the party. My acting skills came in handy as I enthusiastically helped him with choices for filling his suitcase with what he might need at his new residence. I had high hopes that somewhere along the line he would call my bluff on this move and say he was only kidding.

I drove Jenson to his new home and took him and his packed suitcase inside. After initial greetings with his friend and mother, whom I'd just seen less than an hour earlier at the party, I hugged my son and told him, "I love you, and I'm going to miss you sooooo much." Then I turned and began walking out the front door. He promptly burst into tears and declared, "I don't want to live here. I want to go home with you," while his four-year-old feet ran to catch up with me.

To the best of my knowledge, there were no more audible threats to live elsewhere again. However, who knows what was going on in that head of his when he was mad at us in future years?

I don't know if this was an appropriate parenting move or not, but it got the desired result without raising my voice, getting angry, or disciplining Jenson. He was the one who ultimately got to choose what he wanted, and this became a really funny story to laugh about with him and tell others in the future. I have to admit, though, he was so stubborn and clever, I wasn't sure if he would crack when I walked out the door of his "new home."

A month or so after Jenson's suicide, our pastor was checking in with me after church. "I haven't talked to you in a while, how are you doing?"

"I don't really know. I guess okay," I replied.

"Just okay?" asked our pastor.

"Well . . . yes . . . maybe not even okay. I'm really struggling with blaming myself and thinking I must be a terrible mother. Why else would Jenson take his life? If I'd been a good mother, he'd still be here."

"Jenson didn't kill himself because of you, but in spite of you," encouraged our pastor, and in the continuous attempt to silence the guilt screaming in my head, those words considerably helped lower the volume of my self-deprecation as a mother, at least for that moment.

This modicum of relief carried me for a while until the voice of blame started in on its binge again. I wondered if that voice would ever be silenced for good. I had my doubts back then.

As I traverse daily life, it's really difficult to see young families composed of two parents and three children out doing fun things and enjoying their time together. It's even more tenuous for my heart when these families are made up of two older boys and one youngest girl like my own. I often see these family troupes out and about during the warm summer months. I pass them hiking on a trail, or see them at a beach, or stand in line behind them at an ice cream stand, or watch them sitting on a blanket at an outdoor concert, and I'm transported to the days of my own family doing those things as a unit of five when my three were young.

The thoughts in my head don't go to good places at these moments. I wonder what lies ahead for these families I'm meeting or watching. I wonder what Brian and I did wrong to incur the outcome of some of our children's choices, especially Jenson's. I wonder why we couldn't see the things we might have done differently so as to have opposite results. I wonder why I thought we were somewhat happy, when we must not have been, because otherwise there would be no suicide in our family. I wonder why I was so blind then, and yet seem to see quite clearly now. I wonder about so very many things, and that wondering sucks me into a darkness of answerless thoughts that are better left alone. But it's not my nature to leave them alone.

So often it's easier to go to these dark places than it is to stay in the light. The darkness seems an inviting punishment for wrong choices in parenting and relationships with my children. When I pass those happy-faced families encountered on my daily travels, I want to go back and have a do-over, knowing all I know now. But do-overs aren't an option—only rescues and redemption, and those come at great cost.

When I'm in one of these bad mindsets, I hear the voices and lies of others filling my brain with accusations that just aren't true. These accusations bring back memories of secondary infertility and people's thoughtless, unsolicited opinions. Bad theology and the consequences of such then move from the hidden corners of my brain to center stage as I ponder my personal choice in the number of children I wanted. This jumble of thoughts adds more layers of noise in my head.

At times like these, Jenson's death seems like a cruel joke or an unjust punishment considering our three-year struggle of trying to conceive him when we so greatly wanted a second child. We waited a long time for him to be a part of our lives and then lost him way too soon. This causes my mind to proceed to incorrect questioning and a loathing that comes from second-guessing; neither of which is healthy or beneficial.

There had been a time, in the middle of trying to conceive baby number two, when I wasn't sure I really wanted more than one child. Was Jenson's death some sort of just desert for that time of thinking one child was quite enough? Had I ever given Jenson reason to feel unwanted and decide it was better for him to exit life?

Before stepping into marriage, I wasn't even sure I wanted any children. Was Jenson's death retribution for my doubts and lack of desire about being a mother? If so, didn't it count that after I became a mother it felt as if I was born to be one? Questions—always more questions—all of them unsolicited—most of them daunting—none of them answered—most of them emanating from very wrong thought patterns.

I can easily point out the falsehood of these hip-hopping thoughts to any other person who might share them with me during their own self-abasement. There are times, though, when my own mind is on a rampage of personal allegations, and for the life of me, I can't rein it in to anything that vaguely resembles truth.

The lies filling my brain drown out the voice of grace. They're far too frequently on continual play, like the mesmerizing melody of a siren's song that promises something worthwhile to the child-loss of my mother-heart. Perhaps I'll find some sort of answer about Jenson's choice if I listen to these words, which, in my weakest moments, seem to sing a sorrowful minor key on repeat in my searching-for-reasons distress.

However, when I actually take time to hear the words and process them through the ever-constant and trustworthy grace of God, I realize how untrue they are. Sometimes the lies win, but those times grow far more infrequent the further I journey from Jenson's suicide. The grace and mercy of God now allow me much more sturdiness and stability in my mental battles than in past years.

With a sigh of relief because of my present relationship with Tyler and Kalina, I currently more frequently think, "Maybe I didn't mess up my children as much as I tell myself I did. Maybe they actually will miss me and utter truthful, loving words when I die. I won't tell them I don't want a funeral."

We parents think we have far more control over our children than we really do. Perhaps our control is more tangible in the lives of our little ones, but it dissipates as our offspring grow older. Yes, we influence them, but they carry the baggage of our parenting mistakes as much as we carry the baggage of our own mother's and father's poor parenting choices. We can argue nature versus nurture until we're blue in the face with no clear answer to that conundrum. But the bottom line is that our children are who they are, no matter how much we blame ourselves for their erroneous behavior or pat ourselves on the back for the good they do.

Our offspring are wired a certain way and born with a certain disposition, just as we are and were. I'm not sure it's appropriate to blame ourselves or take as much credit as we like to do. In spite of our foibles and perceived failures, for those of us trying to do our best by raising our children the way we think we should, loving them as we're able and know how, 1 Peter 4:8 in the Weymouth New Testament tells us, "love throws a veil over a multitude of faults," both ours and our children's. Let's breathe a sigh of relief about that and stop beating ourselves up so much. Or am I the only one with this inclination?

"Motherhood isn't just a series of contractions. It's a state of mind. From the moment we know life is inside us, we feel a responsibility to protect and defend that human being. It's a promise we can't keep,"[24] says Erma Bombeck. We think we can protect, guide, and direct our children far more than we really can. We think we can control their environment and circumstances so as to give them a greater hope and future than we had. We think they'll keep listening to us for as long as we keep speaking, but the reality is, they won't.

My children grew up and began making some very distinct choices and decisions contrary to the things they'd been taught and told. I'm not a bad parent because your children behave better than mine do at times. You're not a good parent because your children sometimes make better choices than mine.

So many of us are doing the best we can, trying to do a better job than our own parents did. We really, truly are, and the generational reality is that we can only do so much, and then choices are left up to those bundles of love, energy, blood, and bones birthed out of our own bodies. They'll make decisions that shake us to the core and rock our worlds in ways we never even imagined. They're their own persons with their own personalities and proclivities.

We are not the god in our children's lives we think we are or try to be. I became a much more gracious and loving mother when I accepted my children as they are and stopped trying to make them into what I, or other people, thought they should be. That's God's job, not mine. Love will have the final word, and that final word is not mine.

Sometimes, every single one of us on this spinning planet is only holding on by a thread. We must never think we're better or worse than someone else because of how our children turn out. Our children really aren't about us . . . at all. Even after I say this, though, doubts creep back into my mind and once again lead me to self-blame for Jenson's death. Thankfully, though, I'm learning to lean into grace with myself as much as I am with those whom I especially love.

Certain parenting days are extremely difficult since suicide stole one of my treasures—Jenson's birthday, Jenson's death date, and . . . Mother's Day. Yes indeed, I have no use for Mother's Day, at this point in my life. Tyler and Kalina always treat me well and let me know they love me. Why do I need a special day for that? Mother's Day just reminds me of loss.

I greatly dislike going to church that day and listening to typical messages about what "good" mothers should look like. When preparing sermons for Mother's Day or Father's Day, do pastors ever think about the women and men who've lost children and find it really difficult to sit and listen to words that often bring pain rather than encouragement?

It's hard for me to feel worthy of being honored as a mother when my son chose to leave this world. Jenson's choice seems to somewhat disqualify me for any honors of a mothering job well done. I've heard other suicide-survivor mothers say the same thing.

Yes, I did do some things wrong; every parent does. For those things, I've apologized to my children profusely, to the point where they've said something along the lines of "Mom, stop apologizing. If we think of anything else you've done you need to apologize for, we'll tell you, but otherwise, you've covered everything we can think of."

But, in spite of the things I did wrong as a mother over the years—too much rigidity, not enough grace—too much barking, not enough wagging (as the saying goes)—too much "what will others think?" and not enough "who the heck cares what others think?"—I also did some things right. In family videos Brian took when our children were younger, I often glimpse that better mother, the one I've forgotten.

I see a mother singing, reading, and playing with her children, one who sounds much kinder with them than I remember. I see a mother doing creative and fun activities: one getting down and dirty with her little ones; rolling around and wrestling with them on the floor; making as much noise as possible with rhythm instruments; laughing hysterically while playing on a kitchen floor covered with static-electricity-filled packing peanuts stuck to everything; sledding on snowy hills; covering each other in leaf piles; and all kinds of other funness (a Jenson word).

I sound different than I think I was. Surely my children's choices that I label as wrong or with which I don't agree must be indictments on my mothering. But then I see and hear myself in those family videos, and I wasn't as harsh, or as critical, or as condescending, or as mean, or as unkind, or as demanding, or any host of words we associate with bad mothering. And then, out of the blue, Tyler or Kalina thank me for something I did when they were youngsters, and the sun shines out from behind the clouds of self-doubt.

Maybe, just maybe, I didn't mess up my kids as much as I think I must have, and I really am right about having far less control over how our children turn out than we tell ourselves we do. Maybe, just maybe, the whole nature-versus-nurture conundrum is a bit more random and complicated than we like to think it is. Maybe, just maybe, there is far more messiness and then far more grace than we readily admit or accept.

Maybe, in reality, the guilt and shame that feel so normal proclaiming their words into my head are just more of the lies I've falsely believed because it's easier to blame myself than to forgive myself. As I grow in the resting-grace of Jesus, believing what I see and hear wins out far more often than those lies in my head.

And even though I have those moments of mothering self-condemnation, I also sometimes watch other women's behavior with their children and wonder why it's my son who's dead. At times like these I think I can't possibly be as mean or as controlling as the mother whose actions catch my attention, and yet her child is still alive while mine is ashes in a jar. How can that be?

In the spring after Jenson left us, I went into a convenience store while Kalina waited in the car. Upon entering the door I stopped, dumbstruck, as my eyes pursued a mother and who I assumed was her late-elementary-aged son. Dragging him around the store by the hood of his jacket, she verbally assaulted him with a loud, steady stream of "stupid," "sick of you," "jerk," "idiot," and more. With downcast eyes he cowered before her vocal onslaught of anger and tried to stay upright on his feet.

My body froze by the entrance as I refused to let my throat swallow for fear of vomiting out my internal misery over the scene in front of me. Wanting to intervene, but afraid of the repercussions of what I would say, I turned around, left empty-handed, climbed back into the sanctuary of my car, and burst into tears in front of Kalina. Never once, in all my days, had I ever spoken to any of my children like that.

A year or so later, I was visiting a woman I've shared life with off and on. We were touring her new home and entered her eighteen-year-old son's room. This mother disliked the placement of a small table he'd moved, apparently without either her knowledge or her approval. She questioned its new position, and the son responded with "I like it here, instead." The mother promptly picked up the table and put it back where it had been with "Well, I like it better where it was."

What an odd thing to do, an embarrassment for her son in front of a guest. It was his room; can't a young man just have a table where he wants it? It's his choice, right? Teenagers should be able to move bedroom furniture around to their heart's content, shouldn't they? I know I was controlling at times, but was I *that* controlling?

I live in an urban area; mothers yelling at children or belittling them is a way of life for some in the stores, parking lots, and recreation areas I frequent. Shrill denigration is a regular part of the sounds my ears pick up in public places. When I hear the harsh tones, or see the physical inappropriateness, or listen to the demeaning words, I almost always think, "And I'm the one with the son who took his life. Why?"

There are no answers at those times, just an innermost ache for the children who are listening to the wrath of someone who should never, ever talk to them that way and indignation that these mothers get to have a living, breathing child, in spite of their abusive behavior.

Something to Consider: When I jokingly shared the escapades of my sons cheating on their math assignments with the answer key, the mother to whom I was speaking stated, "My children would never do that. We value honesty too much at our house." Hmm . . . well then . . . I guess we Merriams didn't, right?

Why do we feel the need to say things like this mother said to me? It's so condescending and injurious to relationships. Does any parent feel better after another parent has arrogantly proclaimed that in their face? Do you think I ever wanted to talk to that woman again after she shame-slapped me with her degrading declaration?

We parents need to build each other up. We need to be each other's champions. We need to laugh with each other and cry with each other depending on circumstances. We shouldn't ever say, "My children would never . . . !" because we honestly don't always know what our children would do, or are doing at any particular moment when we aren't with them. We all desperately need grace for, and in, raising our children. Grace drowns out both the voice of parental self-blame and the giving of self-accolades, neither of which is healthy or correct.

I often wonder if Jenson would still be alive if grace had overflowed from my mouth more and I'd listened less to what other parents said was right or wrong.

Learn to ignore those undesirable and arrogant parental voices that don't offer the much-needed grace that builds up rather than tears down. We can very easily beat ourselves up; we don't need others to beat on us, too.

CHAPTER 10

"We Make a Beautiful Pair" (Brian)

Brian has a particular love for the people of Haiti and does a good amount of work in that country. He typically travels down there two or three times a year to work on clean-water projects through Rotary International. Tyler and I have gone with him twice, and Jenson and Kalina once each. Both Brian and I wanted our children to have opportunities for viewing the world outside of their American privilege so they might grow in their compassion for the "least of these" on this planet filled with such great need.

Jenson's time in Haiti happened in March of 2010, after the devastating earthquake destroyed much of that country two months earlier in January. He made friends with several young people in the tent camps down there and did most of Brian's filming to be used for future Rotary water projects. He even spoke in front of three thousand Haitians at a prayer-and-praise memorial service commemorating the two-month anniversary of God's mercy since the earthquake.

In hindsight, Brian and I think being in Haiti at that time was just too much for our sensitive son. Jenson would speak very little about that experience after he arrived back home. He typically refused to give reports to anyone who asked about the trip, and if he did say anything it was brief and succinct. I think the carnage, death, and living conditions resulting from the earthquake disturbed him far more than anticipated. It appeared he just didn't want to relive any of it through discussions with those who asked him to tell them about the destruction he witnessed.

Grief is such a singular and individual journey. A person's proclivity to being highly sensitive doesn't necessarily mean the grief process will be more difficult. I would label myself as such, but not Brian, and yet he struggled far more than I did during the first several months after Jenson's suicide. As a matter of fact, he was in pretty abysmal shape for a long time. He didn't go back to work for at least six weeks, and even then, it was extremely difficult for him to function as the "boss," as was his title.

I know Brian felt a burdensome amount of responsibility for Jenson's death, but none of us blamed him. However, he just couldn't function in our house facing his own grief or seeing suicide written on everything his eyes beheld, so after the memorial service he traveled to Atlanta for a change of scenery with his brother and sister.

Tyler went back to graduate school, and Kalina and I remained home alone. I didn't mind Brian leaving for some time away; I certainly felt no sense of abandonment. Somehow it just seemed clear each of us needed to do whatever was crucial for surviving those long, dark, death-filled days of January 2012.

After his return from Atlanta, Brian would end up seeing our hospice counselor on his own more frequently than the two of us together. She was the only one able to help him purposely work on letting go of any culpability he felt for Jenson's suicide. This allowed him to travel through his grief in a less guilt-ridden way. Guilt is such a huge legacy of the suicide-survivor parental journey, so distancing from even a portion of its grip brings a much-needed respite.

During that winter and the early spring months, Brian was especially concerned about Jenson's best friend. This friend was valued and accepted by others because Jenson had included him in relationships and group activities. What would happen to him now that Jenson was gone? In so many ways, Jenson had been the glue that held this friend together in his somewhat dysfunctional life with an absentee father.

Because of this friend's apparent depression, Brian began reaching out to him on a regular basis. It seemed good for both of them. However, sometime in the spring, the friend's father contacted Brian, told him to stay away from his son, and threatened legal action if he didn't do so. How disheartening for my husband. I'm quite sure the son never knew about his father's threats.

It was heart-wrenching to think a father appeared to care so little about his son's welfare that he would limit contact with someone who was trying to help him, especially when that father wasn't around himself. Something that would have been encouraging for Brian, spending time with Jenson's best friend, was taken away by the insecurities of a father who wasn't even present. This was yet another loss in my husband's life. Loss often begets more loss.

While each person grieves individually and independently, the process affects a family as a whole. I felt I carried my family's grief for a very long time, especially Brian's. Many marriages end in divorce after the suicide of a child. Brian is a darker personality than I am, and he was dark for a much longer period of time than I was after Jenson died. This isn't a criticism, at all, just a statement about how differently we're both wired. Brian also struggled with so much self-blame that he could have easily emotionally suffocated from his guilt.

The depth and breadth of Brian's sorrow could have also worn me down to anger and frustration with him, but it didn't. Since we got good, accurate, and wise counsel after Jenson's death, and because both of us read intelligent and compassionate books on grieving, we didn't have any particular expectations for each other. Both of us were actively engaged in our personal and dual grieving, and therefore, we were free to do so as needed. There was never a time when one of us told the other we needed to "get over it," "move on," or "stop being so sad."

I'm extremely grateful for the freedom of this grace shown toward each other. I don't think any spouse is able to heal in a healthy way when there are wrong expectations emanating from the other partner. When we expect someone to grieve the same way we do, we set that person, and our relationship, up for great struggles and potential failure.

About five years out from Jenson's suicide, though, I often felt more tension between Brian and myself than I did when we were closer to his death date. It's hard to articulate why that was, but I have some thoughts on the reasons for that tension.

Part of it may well have been due to me emotionally carrying Brian for so long and the roles we began to play because of that. It seemed Brian was more dependent on my support for his well-being than vice versa. Due to the level of grief in our hearts, I often felt as if I needed to listen more than speak, and therefore, while Brian was articulating what was going on inside of him, and thus processing his grief, I wasn't as much because I was listening rather than verbalizing.

Not only was I listening to Brian; I was also listening to many other people as they processed their own grief from Jenson's death. I listened far more than I talked, which was good for others, but not necessarily for me. For this reason, I especially appreciated the counselors I had, as they were the ones who allowed me to articulate my grief. With most friends and acquaintances, I was typically the ears in conversations.

Another reason I often felt tension between Brian and myself is that he and I look for redemption in somewhat opposite ways. He finds his redemption in large groups, being acquiescent to people in need, helping and maintaining relationships with numerous Haitians, and saying "yes" to projects and activities more often than he says "no."

On the other hand, since I lived most of my life as a people-pleaser before Jenson's death, I've finally learned to say "no," set boundaries, and figure out what's best for my personal well-being. Whereas I used to mostly agree with Brian, now I more frequently challenge his decisions and voice my point of view when asked or when I see the need arise. I also prefer spending one-on-one time with an individual and find large-group activities tedious, tiring, and taxing.

I can't change my husband any more than he can change me. I need to give him the freedom to find redemption the way he sees fit, and he needs to afford me the same consideration, even when it's grueling to try to figure out a balance between the two of us at times. Difficulties arise when our ways of coping collide and we expect the other to understand.

Conflict emerges in different ways than it did before Jenson's death, and, therefore, it seems we need the grace of Jesus even more in our ever-evolving, give-and-take marriage relationship. It's sometimes a dance of unknowns where we get the steps wrong. But it seems much of life is like that anyway, so why should we be surprised when we skip a beat in the music of our marriage waltz?

Jenson's death redefined the playing field of Brian's and my relationship, and it takes commitment to live with the new parameters. Love covers much, but love has occasional moments of running on empty when two hearts have been torn apart over the death of a child. We love, we change the steps, we trip over each other's feet, we become baffled with each other, we sense God's grace, and we return to our love and the discernment of the altered footwork to the dance of our new verity. Grief transmutes normal.

Something to Consider: Grieving spouses need to extend much grace to each other after their child chooses suicide. They need to cling together in their pain and at the same time allow for individual ways of healing. They will seldom be consistently grieving in the same manner at the same time. Therefore, one may appear healthier at times, but it's typically a shifting of steps forward and steps backward for both, no matter which spouse may appear "better" at any given moment.

Our personalities determine much of what our grief walk will look like. One walk is not necessarily better and the other worse; it's just what it is and changes from day to day. Sometimes we can't see how our grief journeys balance each other out until we're several years down the road from the epicenter of our trauma.

Great quantities of patience and love are required for walking the parental suicide-survivor road as a couple, but even then there may be doubts. Hold on to each other as tightly as possible; it's a roller-coaster ride where if one falls out of the car the other has to be the hand that grabs so as to keep the faller from hitting the ground at full gravitational grief speed. This is no simple or easy task at times, but it can be done, and it's worth the fight for your relationship of love.

CHAPTER 11

"Let Me Entertain You"
(Socializing)

Jenson was my one child who didn't perpetually ask to have friends over. He played well by himself and wasn't a social animal like his siblings. When he did pick friends, though, they were far too often the wild, mean-spirited, poorly behaved boys. Why my kindest child gravitated toward kids like this is a mystery to me, but he frequently got in trouble with his friends just by association. Well . . . and because Jenson was so creative in his mischief. Neither he nor most of his friends were particularly good influences on each other in their younger years.

This propensity toward hanging with the "bad boys" lasted until he moved into his teens. By then, he was choosing quieter, less difficult or aggressive friends, and it was indeed a relief for his mother. I have to say that by high school almost all Jenson's friends were enjoyable and delightful, whether male or female. And although gregarious in group settings, he kept his intimate friends to a minimum. True to his introverted self, Jenson typically socialized best in small lots.

Since his suicide, socializing has become a somewhat per-plexing and unsettling activity for me, no matter what size the encompassed number. There are the people with whom I'm close, comfortable, and safe, and whom I enjoy being with; this is a limited number. Those in this group are special treasures to my heart.

There are new people I meet, the ones with whom I fre-quently play the waiting game of "Hmm . . . how uncomfort-able will you become when you learn of Jenson's suicide?" This topic typically follows specific questions about my children after we've covered the tiresome question "What do you do?" "Let's see . . . I do a lot of things; which one do you want to know about?"

Then there's an extremely large circle of acquaintances, the largest group of all, with whom I occasionally socialize in a variety of settings. This is the perplexing category I haven't fig-ured out how to define. These people almost always know about Jenson's suicide, and yet too many of them talk nonstop about themselves and ask me no personal questions whatsoever.

I haven't figured out if they do this because they're self-absorbed and non-engaging conversationalists, or if the truth of Jenson makes them uncomfortable and nervous so they shy away from talking about my personal life. Perhaps their individual anxiety over my reality is assuaged by their endless rambling about themselves. Whatever their reasons for being self-absorbed, it's typically tiring and draining and not par-ticularly pleasurable to spend a lengthy amount of time with these people.

It doesn't frustrate me to lend an ear to the struggles and woes of good or close friends. I count it a privilege to listen well and be an encouragement to them without passing judgment. However, I'm not typically as charitable with strangers or acquaintances I don't know well. Whereas years ago I wouldn't have minded listening as much as I do now, my tolerance for such has been redefined by my own tragedy. Chattering about minutiae has become wearying to my soul, and I'm now much less willing to be pulled into the drama of those with whom I have little or no relationship.

In spite of this, though, I've become a more obvious go-to for acquaintances with a great need to talk about themselves and their difficulties. Jenson's suicide has redressed the balance of endless problem-sharing from people who don't know me well, but are aware of my loss. Something about my circumstances seems to say to them, "Here's someone who will listen to all I have to say about my own issues."

This is often taxing and has caused me to become more introverted, especially in large-group settings with people I don't know well. I really want to be there for friends and for those with whom I choose kinship, but not necessarily for everyone else, unless their heartache speaks to me personally and I choose to enter their pain with them. Consequently, I think I'm less gregarious and outgoing than I once was.

Even before Jenson died, throughout my entire adult life, far too many people have overshared with me on a fairly regular basis. It doesn't seem to matter whether I know someone or not, as people who just happen to be standing near me in line at a store or other places begin talking to me about themselves and telling me their life circumstances—even when I haven't asked.

My children have told me they learned not to make eye contact with strangers because they saw how many people ended up starting conversations with me and telling me their life story after I smiled at them. When I come home and mention to Brian an unsolicited parley I had somewhere he almost always says, "You made eye contact and smiled, didn't you?" Actually, Brian spiritualizes this and says these people probably tell me things because they see Jesus in me. Hmm . . . I'm not so sure about that.

Sometimes I'm able to listen to strangers' and acquaintances' endless talking much more patiently than I am at other times. Much of my forbearance depends on where I am mentally and emotionally at a particular moment. When I'm not in a good internal place, I'm resentful of jabbering. How rude of me is that—not much like Jesus, right?

At these moments I'm typically tired and depleted, and listening to someone who seems to think they are the only one with concerns and life complications grates on my emotional fortitude. I'm intolerant and want to get away as fast as possible. Although it's not obvious, I'm sizing up the room, the other people in close proximity, or my need to go to the bathroom so as to make a quick exit from feeling trapped by someone's chattering mouth. Yep, sounds just like Jesus—*not*—but at that moment, I don't think I even care. "Jesus, please forgive me for my lack of tenacity."

Meeting someone for the first time is usually the most unnerving if the introductory conversation moves to questions about children or my immediate family. When we begin talking about our lives, the topic of parenting almost always comes up if the other person is a parent, too. This typically leads to the number of children we have and then on to the inevitable questions of how old they are and what they do.

What do I say? If I choose to be honest about having three children, the unavoidable query of ages and job choices comes next. My reality is that I have one oldest child, one youngest child, and a dead middle child whose age is younger than his little sister's present age. The telling of this brings about that ever-present puzzled look and questioning "Oh?" from my listener and then my perplexity about what to say next.

However, if I say I only have two children, that's a lie and seems disloyal to Jenson who, although no longer present in body, is one of those three much-loved and cherished creations birthed from my own body. If I say Jenson was eighteen when he died, the next customary question is how he died. When the word *suicide* or phrase *he took his life* is mentioned the discomfort of the questioner becomes palpable.

I want to speak the truth. I'm not ashamed of Jenson's death by suicide. It's the person asking questions who becomes uncomfortable with the truth of my life. I don't want to hide anything, and I'm not looking for pity or sympathy. I don't want to cause them discomfort either, though, so this whole topic of family size or jobs becomes a person-by-person decision based on circumstances and my discernment of the respective doggedness of the one asking me questions.

I have a dear friend whose state trooper son died in the line of duty, and we were talking about this very subject of what we say when people ask us how many children we have. This friend gets my loss and pain over the death of a much-loved son. She's always loving and gracious with me and treats my pain no differently than her own. But when a state trooper dies in the line of duty, he dies a hero's death. No matter how heart-wrenching a hero's death is, it's never embarrassing, or shaming, or scandalous. It's a hero's death and will always be viewed as such.

A suicide changes the rules of a death. There's nothing heroic about it, or at least that's what most people believe. The legacy of a hero's death is vastly different from the legacy of a suicide death. The topic of children takes a very different course when the knowledge of a hero's death is shared. The listener's facial expressions and tone of voice are exceedingly different when asking questions about a suicide death compared to a hero's death. But loss is loss whether someone was a hero or not. However, my guess is that my friend, the state trooper's mother, doesn't spend as much time negotiating conversations as I do. My son wasn't considered a hero.

I've become very adept at turning conversations back to the other person when I just don't want to answer more inquiries or I'm somewhat apprehensive about where the exchange is headed. This is actually fairly easy, because the majority of people are really glad to talk about themselves. Perhaps this makes me sound manipulative, but I simply see it as maneuvering away from yet another unpleasant situation or dialogue. Surviving grief requires we develop coping methods for our well-being, and conversational turnarounds often allow for more comfortable interchanges for both parties.

During the first couple of years after Jenson's death, there were a goodly number of people who told me they'd either like to get together with me for lunch or have Brian and me over for dinner some evening. It's perplexing, though, that these people never followed through or contacted me to put an actual date on the calendar. I might be misinterpreting their actions, but their lack of follow-through on these social suggestions tells me we weren't important enough for their time investment, or they were just being polite and had no intention of spending time with us together or me separately, or perhaps they had no idea what to say and simply blurted out something that they later regretted when realizing spending time with us would be unacceptable or uncomfortable under the circumstances of a suicide.

By now, these people have probably all forgotten their initial invitations, but I haven't. As much as I try to forget, it makes certain associations uncomfortable for me, especially when the invitation was spoken more than once. Sometimes it's easier to distance myself from particular people rather than to see them all smiles and greetings to me and remember they never pursued me after suggesting we get together. Their actions tell me that neither Brian nor I were genuinely important to them or that their perceived distress over spending time with us was greater than their actual desire to breathe compassion into our broken souls.

Even though neither of these may be true, because they didn't follow through with an actual date, their silence over it speaks volumes in my grieving imagination. When it comes to things like suicide, silence from anyone is usually interpreted as rejection. It's pretty much black-and-white for those of us who are survivors, even though the other person might have simply forgotten what they said. Silence holds a huge potential for misinterpretation to those with a broken heart.

My dear husband does insurance risk management for a living. Risk management refers to the practice of identifying potential risks in advance, analyzing them, and taking precautionary steps to reduce or curb the risk. Brian knows way more than the average person regarding this subject and teaches about it because he's an expert in the field.

We were talking about the different people who either are no longer in our lives or who handle us and our grief with great care and aplomb. Brian uses the terms risk-aversion and risk-tolerance in regard to how others deal with us so differently. The people labeled risk-averse are those who are afraid of risk, so they avoid it. Those labeled risk-tolerant are the ones who are willing to take a risk.

The people who walked away from us, or eschew us, or act extremely uncomfortable around us, or make it a point to no longer spend time with us are the people who have a risk-aversion. Those who ask how we really are, listen to us without giving their opinions, seek us out to spend time with us, or invest their hearts in us are the risk-tolerant people. Jesus was the perfect, ultimate risk-tolerant person, and we're all called to be like Him. The people who didn't seek us out after initiating getting together aren't the ones who are like Jesus in this regard.

I actually don't mind that those who have risk-aversion are no longer in our lives; they make me rather uncomfortable, and, most likely, vice versa. But those who are risk-tolerant are the hands and feet of Jesus to my heart and soul, and for them I'm ever grateful. For the most part, pursuing someone makes them feel valued and loved. It's easy to walk away, but it takes a lot more effort, fortitude, and courage to stay. I have great esteem for the ones who stayed.

As time moves further away from December 23, 2011, there are those whom we don't see frequently who forget Jenson took his life. This makes spending time with these particular people more difficult than usual. When one of these people says anything that demonstrates they forgot about his suicide, I can see the realization on their face after they've said something inappropriate, looked at me, and only then remembered my loss. They're obviously uncomfortable but don't apologize or say anything in reference to their unsuitable remark.

Some joke about killing themselves if something or someone doesn't stop doing whatever it is that annoys them. There are also the jokes told about someone taking their life, with their suicide being the punch line. None of these things are funny. They may well have been before suicide claimed a life I love, but my sense of humor has most certainly been redefined about death.

I would respect someone so much more if they apologized for their faux pas once the reality and memory of my loss dawned on them. I'm not angry these things happen. I'm only sad that one more person has forgotten my Jenson.

As a matter of fact, people who now meet us for the first time, or see us in passing, would never know of our casualty or the hole Jenson's suicide has left in our hearts. By God's grace we live most of our days like everyone around us, functioning, competent, and unassuming. Our terrible tragedy is no longer written all over our faces, so our countenances don't give glimpses into the depths of our hearts. Those who don't know us appear to take us as we are, and those who do know and love us no longer seem to tiptoe around our emotional suicide-upheaval.

Perhaps, because we do appear to be doing well, this is why many forget about Jenson's death and our loss. We're no longer just on the edge of falling apart or barely holding it together. We don't have to desperately work to keep control of ourselves so as not to make others regret spending time or socializing with us.

In spite of everything, we pretty much now function as normally and ordinarily as the rest of you in our day-to-day living. Still, I'm incredibly grateful for those who know of our loss and choose a relationship anyway. They're of far greater value to my heart than those who walked away or didn't pursue us when given the opportunity.

Something to Consider: If you want to spend time with someone who is grieving, then do so. If you don't, then don't. It's really okay not to be with them. They're not counting on you if you never mentioned spending time with them in the first place.

However, if you verbalize that you want to spend time with someone and say, "Let's get together," or "We'd love to have you over for dinner," or "I'd love to meet you for lunch," then follow through by giving the grieving person an actual date to which they may agree or offer an alternative. A verbal invitation followed by silence is a hurtful thing. What would you think if that happened?

Grace doesn't need to look like an invitation, but it most certainly shouldn't look like silence after your spoken suggestion of a get-together. If you don't want to spend time with someone, then don't invite them in the first place. There will be no expectations, which is more peaceful for both parties.

CHAPTER 12

"Can You Find It in Your Heart?" (Talking About Jenson)

Jenson was not my most talkative child at any particular age in his short life. He was a listener and observer, artistic to the core. He was not the one drawing attention to himself in group settings, even with his great sense of humor. His entertaining comments were made quietly, under his breath, to whoever was sitting next to him. Then, while that person laughed hysterically, Jenson sat with an unassuming expression, pretending he had no clue what was so funny while he quietly doodled in the notebook that always appeared attached to his hand.

When Brian took him to father-son retreats, he hung back with his ears glued to the conversations of the men instead of running around outside in crazy paintball games with the teens. He would later return home with delightful, amusing, tell-all caricatures of several of the males, both old and young, who attended those retreats.

In group settings, he wouldn't raise his hand when an answer was required, but if asked for one, he almost always responded correctly. And when behind the camera giving directions for his filmmaking endeavors, he knew exactly what he wanted and made his requests concisely, without being verbose or endlessly detailed for no apparent reason. Jenson wasn't one to waste words unnecessarily.

Always humble about the awards he received, he seldom told others about them after the ceremonies. I never heard him speaking to anyone about his accomplishments unless he was asked to do so. He found bragging, boasting, and tooting your own horn demonstrations of the narcissistic tendencies he so hated in others.

In addition to his nomination for Outstanding Actor for his portrayal of Tevye, Jenson also received numerous awards for his cartoons in the *Student Gazette*, the yearly Schenectady newspaper competition for school-age youngsters in various categories of newspaper publishing. He entered this competition each year from fifth grade until he graduated from high school and won first place for his comic strips/cartoons every year save one, when he came in second. His film awards were numerous, too, after he began making movies and sending them to film festivals and competitions.

Jenson took Schenectady County Community College classes for his entire senior year of high school. One of those classes was college composition, a class heavy on writing and the skills that accompany it. At the end of the semester, he received an award for a paper he'd written for that class. He was still too young to be matriculated but was the one student who received this particular achievement that year. In his perpetual humility about his accomplishments, I'm not sure he even talked to anyone about this unique honor.

Within the year after Jenson's death, Kalina began referring to us as "the people *to* whom we do not speak," a play on the phrase "the people of whom we do not speak" from the movie *The Village*, a favorite of Jenson's and the rest of our family. Not only did we become those "people to whom we do not speak," but a large number of friends and acquaintances would stop talking about Jenson and never mention his name to us again.

In less than six months after his death, his sixteen-year-old girlfriend moved on to a new boyfriend, resulting in marriage and a baby in fewer years than I care to count. Except for a scribbled note on a family Christmas card, we've not heard one single word from Jenson's best friend in several years. Although a very small number of his friends still post on his Facebook page on his birthday and death date, some of his closest friends have become completely silent.

Why, though, would I expect anything different? I don't know if the old adage "Time heals all wounds" is true, but the one about "time marching on" certainly appears to be so, and people march along with it, on to their next phase of life, their next adventure, their next cause, their next trouble, or their next needy person. I don't blame them; this is human nature, and I probably used to do the same thing. When we have satiated our own personal interest, we move on to the next calamity that piques our curiosity.

However, for those of us who've lost a child, even though time continues to march on and we get dragged along with it, we're doing so with a broken heart, a hole in our lives, an empty place at our once full holiday table, and the diminishing essence and DNA from that dear child we loved so completely. We're never fully whole again; part of our heart is missing from daily life, and most everything is a continual reminder of that fact. Others get to move on, but we don't because we now have one foot in Heaven rather than two feet on earth.

It's almost as if we live in three different worlds all at the same time: the past where Jenson was, the present where we are but he isn't, and our Heavenly future where he is but we are not. "Moving on" isn't an option for us like it is for others, because every picture of our family of five is a reminder that someone is missing since we're now only four. There will never be another family photo taken of "all five of us." Why didn't I get one taken more frequently?

Grief and recovery are such singularly personal journeys that others need to be able to respond in a variety of ways if they want to provide loving and compassionate support to those on the journey. Some who've lost a child to suicide may not like to speak of their dead child, but . . . **I like to talk about Jenson.** I love displaying his pictures, wearing a ring with his name on it, and having people ask me about his initials tattooed on my forearm. A very small and loving portion of my close friends and extended family members seem to be okay with me talking about Jenson. They talk about him, too, and I really, really like that.

When these dear people share Jenson memories with me, my heart sings because I may have forgotten that particular story or not even known it in the first place. If it's a funny story, amusement over the delight Jenson brought to others raises my level of joy. If it's a tale of how kind he was, my mother-heart pride swells over another time he brought comfort and goodwill to someone who so needed it at a particular moment. The light of grace wins out in these talking-about-Jenson moments as the heaviness of grief is banished by rejoicing in my son.

However, there are those whose look of discomfort is unmistakable when I mention his name. I haven't figured out if it's Jenson being dead that makes these people uneasy or if it's because he took his life. But the look on their faces—wide eyes, furrowed brow, visible angular facial distress, pursing of lips—then makes me uncomfortable, too, and I want to say, "It's tough for you if you don't like me talking about my dead son, or that you don't know what to say, but this isn't about you, so deal with it." I don't say that, though, because that would be rude and unkind and make both of us feel even more uncomfortable. Plus, there's no way to say that and sound like Jesus.

However, these thoughts frequently take up residency in my brain space as they float around trying to plumb the depths of my friendships. We don't do grief well in the USA or the evangelical body of the church. The person who is grieving has to continuously adjust their personal pain so as not to make others uncomfortable. My grief is often about how someone else feels, rather than how I feel. I'm always extremely grateful for friends who allow me the honesty and transparency of my own sorrow over the loss of Jenson. They neither put constraints nor time limits on what I want to say about my dead son.

Not only are many people uncomfortable talking about Jenson, but a very large number never uttered his name, ever again. This adds greater hurt to my heart and makes it seem as if they're denying he ever existed. In *The One-Year Book of Hope*, Nancy Guthrie shares what she learned from a grieving friend: "she shared with me one of the most painful aspects of losing her son. It was when people didn't say anything to her after her son died. She said, 'I wanted to tell them, "How could you add to my pain by ignoring it?"'"[25] That's how I feel when people won't speak Jenson's name or join me in my discussion when I mention him. My thoughts say, "You're ignoring my pain and, therefore, ignoring my son."

Over and over again, I find I'm the one trying to make other people feel less unsettled when they're uneasy over something I've said about Jenson. Rather than joining me in my conversation about him, they just stare at me in awkward silence. At moments like this, I'm the one who takes responsibility for either moving the exchange forward or just staring back in some sort of odd waiting game of "who'll speak first." I don't like that game, though. It's too much work for absolutely no fun at all, and there really isn't a winner.

If that awkward silence shows up while we're eating, we can just look down at our plates and stuff more food in our mouths. If we're out and about, I can point out something in our general vicinity that might claim our attention instead of what I've just said about Jenson. If we're joking about something, I can rack my brain for another anecdote that might bring a bit of uncomfortable laughter after a quick change of subject.

But what would really be kind is if the awkward silence were ushered away by the person I'm talking to simply by them taking their comfort-level cue from me, instead of the other way around. I listen to all the things they want to talk about. I would love the same courtesy extended to me when I mention Jenson.

There are times in verbal discourse or in writing when I can sense his unspoken name hanging in the air like untouched static electricity, not discharged due to lack of contact. I've concluded people assume they're doing us a kindness by not using the name of our dead son; they don't want to present more grief to our hearts. Plus, it's really unpleasant for them to bring up his name because they, themselves, don't want to feel the uncomfortable sensation of not knowing what to say.

We so appreciate people who take the risk to talk about Jenson, because it verbally validates his continual existence in our lives now that we no longer have his physical presence. His name spoken from the lips of others is the tangible evidence that he isn't forgotten by those people any more than he could ever possibly be forgotten by us.

Brian and I think about Jenson every single day whether people mention him or not. It's not as if when someone doesn't speak his name we don't think about him. He continues to be, and always will be, one of the three prominent treasures of our hearts. Those who actually make the effort to talk to us about him give us an extraordinarily generous gift very few bestow upon us.

I really wish people would get over not knowing what to say and say something that acknowledges Jenson was once a living, breathing, precious person in my life. At least speak his name out loud so I can hear it from someplace other than my own mouth. If I say something about him, or initiate a conversation, then don't make it about your level of comfort; join me in my memories and stories. Allow yourself to be vulnerable. That's love, mercy, compassion, kindness, and commiseration.

Something to Consider: When you take time to sit in the ashes with a grieving parent, let them guide the conversation. If they want to tell you stories about their child, take your cues from them; listen and ask questions. If they just want to sit quietly, rest in the silence with them, and don't allow the air to be filled with your uneasiness. Choose to speak their child's name, and notice how their body reacts; then either continue or discontinue your dialogue by what the parent's body language is telling you. Sometimes the greatest gift of grace you can give to a grieving parent is to get out of your comfort zone and allow that parent to discuss their dead.

CHAPTER 13

"My Defenses Are Down"
(Hurtful)

On the day after that death that changed us forever, one of the men who came to sit with Brian in his shock and shattered-by-suicide aftermath came downstairs from Jenson's room to talk with me for a bit. He found me sitting alone on our couch, my mind staring into a space of confusion and uncertainty. He sat down and began discussing the masks and posters that hung on the walls in Jenson's room.

Our son was a lover of horror movies, scary books, and anything that raised the hair on the back of his neck. That man let me know how troubling he found those things in the bedroom, and that he would not have let his own children possess such items. Whenever the words "I would never let my children . . ." leave the mouth of another parent, you can be sure you're in for some shame-slapping upside the head. However, with the passing of time, I now assume he was expressing his distress and not actually blaming us, but that's certainly not where my mind went the day after Jenson's suicide.

My roaring guilt, present without his help, rose to a volume that silenced the words continuing to come out of his mouth which I could still see moving. However, I'd ceased listening as my brain processed the personal accusations circling on the hamster wheel of my mind. Why didn't I just tell him to stop and be gone—because I had to be polite, of course. Yes, even in heart-wrenching pain, I couldn't be anything but polite, right?

My guess is Jenson's death was the first time most of the people we knew had direct experience with a suicide, including that man sitting next to me in our living room the day after our hearts were ripped out. Suicide was certainly not discussed in churches or the homeschool community at that time. And due to a lack of knowledge about it, some people seemed to make the choice to say whatever they wanted no matter how it affected us. But since I didn't know how to articulate the increased damage that man's words caused me at that moment, I sat in silence with my own thoughts of personal indictment while he continued speaking.

I should have stood up for myself more during the earlier years of my all-encompassing Jenson-suicide grief when people said such very inappropriate things that would've been better left unspoken. People need to know when the things they say or do cause greater hurt than what is already coursing through the melancholy-filled veins of a brokenhearted parent.

If I'd spoken up, I might have moved to forgiveness sooner. Although forgiveness eventually came in these verbal injuries I mention, it took longer than it probably would've had I not buried the hurt under my grief. Acknowledgment opens the door to letting go.

Fast-forward a few months to our *Seussical: The Musical* program just about ready to go to print at the beginning of May 2012. The cast members wanted the show to be performed in memory of Jenson. However, one of the extremely conservative, uptight cast mothers didn't think this was appropriate and took issue with it. Yet again, more hurt.

She thought performing the show in his memory would make it sound as if suicide was acceptable. What?! How does that in any way, shape, or form make suicide sound acceptable? Thankfully, my producer intervened and pointed out that the teens made the choice about the program, and never once had I or anyone else ever given a hint of suggesting the way Jenson died was "okay." My producer took good care of me that winter.

When I spoke to my grief counselor about this, she said the mother was most likely reacting out of her personal fear for her daughters. If our family, or anyone else, had been saying Jenson's suicide was acceptable, then that might encourage other teens to take their own lives, too. I understood the mother's fear, if that was what it really was, but it was just one more thing to have to deal with from other people who weren't particularly gracious or kind with their confrontational accusations.

Suicide frequently pushes others into cluelessness about how to ask the less accusatory questions. It would've been so much easier had the disturbed mother not been censorious and given us the benefit of the doubt that we weren't stamping approval upon Jenson's method of death. It's so easy to go to the wrong story, or change the facts to fit the narrative. I do this myself, but hopefully not as often as before Jenson died.

Most likely, the great majority of people don't think about how their words affect others. No one gets up in the morning and decides they'll make statements that bring hurt or question to the hearts and minds of another person. Words just flow out of mouths and take on a life of their own as they become manipulated puppets on the strings of our endless, streaming thoughts, fears, and concerns. Everyone processes life events so differently.

I don't want to hurt those who've hurt me, but I do desire for people to be aware their words have consequences upon the hearts and minds of others. The ending of the old adage ". . . but words will never hurt me" is a big fat lie. Words have the power to be a balm to our souls or the infection that keeps our wounds from healing. Even now, ten years down the road from Jenson's suicide, I remember and am acutely aware of not only the things I'm mentioning but the many other inappropriate things that have been said in the ensuing time since his death.

I don't believe the intentions behind any specific words were mean-spirited or purposely heartless, but the pain thrust upon my wounded soul, and those of my dear family members, is just as great as if the goal was to cause damage. What's most perplexing, though, is that almost all the hurt happened within church settings or Christian organizations.

I was attending a women's Sunday-school class at our church a year or so after Jenson's death. At first, it felt fairly safe to be there since church continued to be difficult for me at that time. I don't even remember the theme of the class, but one Sunday we were talking about grief and how we view God in the midst of our suffering.

"So what helps you in your grief over the difficulties in your life?" asked our teacher. Her question was met with silence. No one said anything, but it felt as if the other women were giving me side glances of anticipation.

She tried another approach. "Do you like to talk about your grief or keep it to yourself?"

Silence continued.

"I lost my sister to suicide when we were both teenagers, but I don't like to talk about it," said the older woman sitting next to me, obviously uncomfortable with the lingering hush.

The other women looked at her with furrowed brows and looks of compassion on their faces as the teacher stated, "I'm sorry."

Now I found the quiet awkward, so I spoke up. "I like to talk about Jenson." All the women in the class knew my story and turned their attention to me.

"Why?" asked my sister-suicide-surviving neighbor in an incredulous tone of voice.

"Well, it makes it seem like he continues to be the huge part of my life that he actually is. It doesn't make me sad to talk about him. I want to talk about him." And I went on to briefly say a few more things about my grief journey.

Now the teacher joined the conversation again and spoke directly to me. "I find your journey so interesting. Don't you feel privileged and honored that God would entrust you with the special gift of bearing Jenson's suicide?"

I stared at her, dumbstruck, as I contemplated her words. "What the . . . ?" was the question in my mind. "Did she really ask me what I think she just asked?" stated my mind to itself. "I can't believe she put me on the spot by saying this in front of the other women—Jenson's suicide a special gift from God?" My mind was still carrying on the dialogue with itself.

In response to her question, I lowered my gaze and mumbled something but have absolutely no memory of what it was. And all the other women in the class just let me sit with their silence.

Later, I wished I'd thought to ask the teacher which one of her daughters she would choose to die by suicide so she could have the same privilege and gift she thinks God commended to me. Her naivete was bewildering, the smile on her face astonishing, her theology most disturbing. I can't decide which is sadder, that people say such hurtful things or that they don't even realize what they're saying.

In the spring of 2014, I was directing the musical *Annie* for our homeschool co-op and had gone to a church to work with a teen who was stepping into a role for someone dropping out due to medical problems. After I was done with my rehearsal, a past acquaintance came up to speak with me. I'd neither seen nor spoken with this woman since Jenson died, although I'm sure she saw me in the grocery store the year after his suicide but turned around and walked away before any dialogue could ensue. I'd recognized her, but she was gone before my mouth even opened to say "Hi."

She'd even left a voice mail on my phone with a question about homeschooling but said nothing of Jenson or her being sorry for my loss when leaving that message less than two years after he died. She knew about his death. Everyone at her church knew about it.

This woman now apologized for ignoring me after Jenson's suicide and told me she just couldn't reach out to me because of her youngest daughter's mental-health issues and how troubling they were to deal with on a regular basis. She talked on and on about her daughter's depression and suicide attempts and then finally said to me, "I don't mean to compare, but you have no idea how hard it is to drive away from leaving your daughter in a lockdown mental-health facility."

There were those words I'd heard from other people: "I don't mean to compare, but . . ." Those are heartless words that insinuate someone else's pain is worse than yours. Those words should never, ever be spoken to a grieving parent, because they blatantly state the person is, in truth, comparing.

As I drove home, I thought had I actually wanted to compare difficult circumstances, I could've responded with "Well, okay, but you have no idea how hard it is to see your dead son taken out of your house in a body bag!" Comparison destroys relationships, and it never, ever looks like charity.

Another time, after my singing a solo in our summer church, a woman came up to me and told me God must have taken Jenson because He knew I was strong enough to deal with it and blah, blah, blah, since "He doesn't give us any more than we can bear." She went on to tell me God was honoring my strength by allowing me to suffer loss.

Really?! It didn't feel like anything, whatsoever, close to a special honor. I didn't want my strength honored like that. I'd rather be weak and have Jenson back, but that's not an option.

Was she also saying that anyone who hasn't suffered the loss of a child isn't as strong as I am? I'm then supposed to say, "Gosh, God, I sure am glad I'm so strong so you decided to take my son"? Or how about "I'm so glad I'm stronger than all the rest of you who have children who are still alive"? This whole proposal of "If I wasn't strong enough, God wouldn't . . ." sounds a bit like deceptive, self-justified arrogance covering up brokenhearted regret or an unwillingness to say, "God, this death, or disease, or earthquake, or fire, or accident, or whatever, is just plain wrong."

This whole idea of God not giving us more than we can handle is taken from 1 Corinthians 10:13 and is a verse I believe we've gravely misinterpreted. It's talking about temptation, not about God honoring strength by allowing us to suffer. That's just a mistaken way to view a loving God. As I read that verse, the correct interpretation seems to be that God will help us deal with the difficulties that come our way. That takes the blame off God and promises His help with the onerousness of our life struggles. That sounds way more like love and grace.

Several years after Jenson's death, another woman would bring up the Bible verses of Luke 14:26 and Matthew 10:37, where we're told to hate our family members, or not love them more than God, because then we're not worthy of following Jesus. This was shared with me after she told me she'd been thinking about Jenson's suicide and why it might have happened. If she was trying to comfort me, this was a huge fail on her part, because all this sounded like was that she was telling me I must have loved Jenson more than God, and that's why God took him. How messed up is that?!

The ramifications of this insinuation are astoundingly troubling. If her conclusion is true, then I must not love Brian, Tyler, or Kalina as much as I loved Jenson, because they're still living. Heck, I must have even loved our cat more than my three living family members, because she died, and they haven't.

Or this particular woman's words could make me think God was so jealous of my love for Jenson, He couldn't stand the competition so He took my younger son out of the game. Yes, that's certainly a sagacious way to guarantee you have a first-place spot in someone's heart—kill off the competition.

Does that in any way, shape, or form sound like Jesus? I know the words in Luke 14 and Matthew 10 were spoken directly out of His mouth, but we need to be really, really careful how we translate those words to the ears and hearts of others. They don't mean what this woman was implying. We must never suggest, to anyone, no matter what the death circumstances are, that God took a person out of our life because we loved them more than we love Him.

God is not a sadistic narcissist who doesn't want us to love anyone else. He's an excruciatingly and abundantly loving Father who cares for us so much He let His own Son die so we didn't have to spend our whole lives wallowing in the excrement of our personal sins. That most certainly doesn't sound like someone who needs to kill off the competition.

Brian's experiences with people's good intentions but complete lack of understanding and common sense were often similar to mine. It was somewhere around the second anniversary of Jenson's death, and he and I were walking into the Sunday-morning worship service at our church.

The Elder who was greeting people stopped Brian and asked, "How are you? Are you still struggling, you know, since that thing that happened to your son a couple years ago?"

My husband responded with "Hell yes." "Hell" seems like an acceptable word to use in church, right?

"I understand," said the Elder. "My dad died a little while ago."

"Was your dad elderly, and did you expect him to die?" asked Brian.

"Well, yes, actually."

"Well, my son wasn't elderly, he was eighteen, and we didn't expect him to die, so you don't understand." And Brian followed me to our pew.

First of all, maybe Eldership training should involve a class on how to ask compassionate questions that don't make people wonder about your leadership skills or want to avoid you for the next twenty years of church attendance. Secondly, this Elder was comparing our eighteen-year-old son's suicide to the natural death of an elderly man and stating he understood. I don't think so!

I know the Elder meant well, and I get that he lost his father, but to say what he said demonstrated just how much he didn't comprehend what we were living through. William Ritter, who lost his adult son to a self-inflicted gunshot, wrote, "All loss or bereavement is horrible, but there is a dimension of pain from the death of a child, especially by suicide, that is unique and severe indeed."[26]

Almost every single inappropriate thing that has been said to us by others has come out of the mouths of those claiming to be Christians. No wonder so many people don't want anything to do with Jesus or those of us who profess we know Him. Far too often, we have a propensity for being clueless, hurtful, and really slow learners when it comes to manifestations of love.

We don't regularly make Jesus look good. We who should be the most compassionate, patient, forgiving, grace-filled, tolerant, loving, and more are not. I'm lumping myself right into these indictments because I still have much to learn.

As I think on charity and the words we speak to each other, I'm reminded there are some things that would have been much more loving and comforting to hear than many of the things actually said to us. I've come to some very specific conclusions as to what is helpful to say and what isn't when navigating a dialogue with someone grieving the death of a loved one, especially the suicide of a child.

These following suggestions are far kinder than what Brian and I frequently experienced, but they don't typically occur to a person not walking a path of bereavement:

- Don't use the word "still," as it has no place in the vocabulary uttered to someone who is grieving no matter how long they've been doing so. Ray Pritchard states, "God knows we cannot comfort others by trying to minimize the pain of loneliness and personal anguish."[27] The word "still" always diminishes personal anguish.
- Listen far more than you speak to the person whose heart is broken—this isn't about you but about the person who lost someone.
- Avoid speaking every single platitude you've heard uttered (and I truly mean all of them) and every single scripture verse like Romans 8:28 ("And we know that all things work together for good to those who love the Lord . . .") that people love to quote to those who are suffering, or turning the narrative back to yourself about understanding because your parent, dog, or great-uncle recently died. If you haven't lost a child to death, especially a death by suicide, then you don't understand. Really, I'm serious, you don't understand, and you have no business saying you do and then steering the conversation to your loss.

In regard to platitudes and Romans 8:28, these are unacceptable to quote because they do so much damage to a heart that is already barely beating owing to loss. If the one who is grieving wants to quote a platitude or Romans 8:28, okay, but everyone else should just put a hand over their mouth before something trite comes out. Banal and commonplace clichés have no place in the speech of pain and sorrow. They just raise toxicity levels and make the infection of anguish ooze even more.

When someone quoted Romans 8:28 to me or told me to look for the good that would come out of my tragedy, it wasn't helpful because the pain of losing Jenson was screaming in my heart and brain, and at that moment, no good that might potentially result would be worth the loss. I heard Romans 8:28 so often I wanted to start slapping people who quoted it to me. To this day, I have to make a conscious effort not to dislike that verse when it's used with the mistaken meaning so many inadvertently assign to it because of what I consider an incorrect interpretation.

People's thoughtless and hurtful comments were wearying. It was interesting, though, when after Brian told some people what they said wasn't appreciated, they justified their inappropriateness by stating, "Well, don't my good intentions count for something?" But these same proudly pious evangelicals would be the first to declare God won't let someone into Heaven just because of "good intentions" without having a personal relationship with Jesus. I'm not sure good intentions actually count for all that much, when the end result is more pain.

It's so easy to justify our hurtful words and actions by saying we meant well. Yet a true and loving relationship challenges us to think about the angst we may have caused another person, not try to discredit our wrongdoing by turning it back to our own goodwill about what we said.

As my own dear husband stated in the first several months after our son's death, "I would like something between the silence of God and the prattle of stupid people!" In the early years after Jenson died, I wasn't sure where to find that "something." It's only now, several years away from December 2011, that I'm able to speak up and attempt to point out grievous words from others that would be better left unspoken. It took me a few years to find vocal courage.

Something to Consider: I've come to the conclusion that when the Bible tells us in Ephesians 4:29 to "not let any unwholesome talk come out of [our] mouths," it is most likely not speaking about swearing or dirty jokes—the opposite of what I learned in Sunday school in my younger years. But since I was an obedient, people-pleasing child, I refrained from four-letter words and inappropriate humor. Well, at least until well into my adult years, when I came to the conclusion that God is not nearly as disappointed in potty-mouthed people as I was told He is.

Following the "unwholesome" portion of that verse are the words "but only what is helpful for building others up according to their needs, that it may benefit those who listen." Wow, my Sunday-school teachers left that portion out on a regular basis. The rest of us do, too, but that's the most important part of the whole verse.

The hurtful things we say to grieving people do not build them up in their time of need. Hurtful words aren't beneficial to the listener. It doesn't matter that we meant well if something we said does damage to someone's suffering heart. We absolutely have to think about what we say before we say it to a grieving parent, or to anyone who's grieving, for that matter.

2 John 1:6 states, "His command is that you walk in love." It's not a suggestion; it's not a "perhaps"; it's not a "maybe you should consider"; it's not an "if you feel like it"; it's a command, and those don't leave much room for doubt about

interpretation. When we're walking in love we don't say the things that have been said to Brian and me, no matter what version of the Bible we use.

Love allows grace to speak in the same way that grace allows love to speak. May love and grace rule our tongues far more than what appears to be normal.

CHAPTER 14

"The God-Why-Don't-You-Love-Me Blues"
(Anger with God)

Jenson failed his driver's test the first time he took it, but he didn't seem very upset, at all. He did pass test number two, but none of us wanted to ride with him even when he could officially and legally drive by himself. Nor did Brian or I feel comfortable when Jenson was driving his sister or any of his friends around after that. For being my most focused child, he also ended up being our worst family driver. He was easily preoccupied and distracted while behind the wheel of a car.

He was also a rather angry driver, which was an even greater surprise. Jenson hated when other drivers were thoughtless and rude. Even though he wasn't a really good driver himself, he was a very kind one, with a heightened sense of what people should and shouldn't do when it came to the rules of the highway. I wondered if he would have been consumed by road rage had he not been so loving and considerate. Sometimes anger rears its ugly head when we least suspect it. Driving brought out Jenson's anger in a way nothing else appeared to do.

Jenson's death brought out my own anger, and it surfaced several months after his suicide. Shock would last for about three months, but as it wore off, reality began to dig its sharp talons into the flesh of my torn and bleeding heart. A few months later I didn't just say "I hate you," or "God, I HATE you." No, it wasn't enough just to say either of those. With a vengeance, I clearly and adamantly declared into the night sky, "I HATE YOU, GOD," and I meant it, every single word.

I'm not ashamed of my hostility or my words to God; He can take anything we throw at Him. Why pretend I wasn't angry when He already knew what I was thinking? He's God, for crying out loud; why try to pull off a sham with Him?

Honesty is an amazing burden-lifter and emotional release. Pretending to be better than I was didn't seem like an option for healing. Somehow it was plain to me that if I wanted to move through my grief in the process of healing, I had to be honest with both God and myself. By the time anger hit, I didn't give two hoots what anyone else thought, but I wasn't quite willing to declare to anyone that I hated God. It was my dirty little secret between me and my Maker.

It was around the fifth month after Jenson's suicide when the reality of him never again being on this earth hit me like a gut punch that took my breath away for weeks on end. I felt so lost, alone—totally ignored and abandoned by God. And because of His silence, anger rose like bile in my mouth, and I no longer trusted Him. Ray Pritchard hit the nail on the head with his words: "Of all the things that weigh us down, perhaps no burden is greater than the silence of God."[28]

Darkness hovered over my soul, and the faith that had carried me for the past months ebbed away into a spiritual limbo of wondering why God left me when I needed Him most. This was one of the darkest times for me since the initial shock of Jenson's death.

How could God have so failed me by allowing one of my children to die by suicide? I had a personal relationship with Jesus and had faithfully served Him since the age of fifteen. I'd done what the church told me to do in order to be a "godly" woman, wife, and mother so as to earn favor with Him. I was there when the doors were open; I was a virgin when I got married; I was a faithful wife; I let my husband take the lead; I homeschooled my children; I willingly served the Lord and other people.

I did it all, and yet my kindest, most thoughtful and loving child was dead by his own hand, and God had not stopped him. Why hadn't He done something to prevent Jenson from dying? In her article "The Hard Work of Being Job's Wife," Jenefer Igarashi says, "I understand being so overwhelmed and broken in my circumstances that in my despair—despite claiming Christ and knowing that I belong to Him—my faith has been drained away and I have despised God."[29] Jenefer's words were the reality of my existence at that time; I despised God.

I'd believed the false premise that my faithfulness and obedience to God somehow correlated to the blessings I should and would receive from Him. One of those blessings should have been the safeguarding of my children. "God, I've done my part for almost forty years, and yet *you* failed in executing the protection I expected was a guarantee because of my 'holiness' and 'godliness.'"

I'd been taught guarantees and promises since the age of fifteen, but now doubts about God's faithfulness and trustworthiness consumed my cranium space. Carolyn Custis James declares, "In a way, every grief is two-dimensional—the loss itself along with the nagging thought that it could have been prevented if only God had acted."[30] My doubt was not just a "nagging thought"; it was a roaring allegation against a lifetime spent following God for what now appeared to be no return on investment.

We humans like to package everything up in nice, neat little formulaic boxes. We're so much more secure with guidelines to follow, rules to obey, and lists that keep us on track and make us feel as if we've accomplished the needed tasks for daily living. So many of us feel safer in the boundaries designated by those who propose they know more than we do—our parents, the church at large, theologians, Christian leaders, leaders in general, our government, authors of self-help books, et cetera.

We're uncomfortable standing before God in our spiritual nakedness so He can change us into who He wants us to be rather than who everyone else tells us we should be. We can't see God, so it's difficult to hear Him over all the other talking mouths in our field of vision. It appears less complicated to just listen to the powers that be and assume they know what they're speaking about.

We come up with formulas because following 1+2=3 seems easier than standing face to face with difficult circumstances, our own imperfections, and the flaws of those who share life with us. But life is really terribly muddled, and formulas only work in math, not when we're dealing with flesh-and-blood people. All formulas seem to actually do is add more guilt and shame to our already tenuous lives when we fail at their proper execution and orchestration. I was living that guilt and shame, and it had turned into anger.

Formulas aren't relational. They may work in Fortune 500 companies, but not in families, or friendships, or faith in God, or the death of a loved one. I espoused and followed the formulas I was told would bring happy, healthy, godly children, and yet here I was, living in the aftermath of the suicide of my child who most frequently evidenced Jesus in his heart. Where were the guarantees now? Even more troubling and disheartening, where was God? So much for believing the promised outcome of 3 when 1 is added to 2. In reality, life occurrences play out nothing like an arithmetic equation.

My journal writing began shifting around this time as anger seeped into my thoughts and heart. The recording of events took a back seat to my doubts about God. As my missing of Jenson increased, my caring about God decreased. My journal entries read, "Why would God allow Jenson to die?"; "Why didn't He stop Jenson's death?"; "If He's so loving, why do we now have so much carnage?"; and more. Ray Pritchard writes, "I have come to the conviction that the biggest barrier to faith is life itself."[31]

Life had drawn a line in the sand of my faith, and I had to choose sides. Was I going to walk away from all I'd believed since I was fifteen, or was I going to cross over that line and find out if I had the faith and chutzpah to continue on my grief journey and allow certain theological assumptions to be redefined?

In the deep recesses of my mind I knew I couldn't walk away. In spite of all my anger and doubt, my heart was crying out to God with: "Where else can I go? You are the One who has the words of life" (John 6:68). I stepped over the line toward God and allowed Him to rewire my faulty faith.

Something to Consider: I think we sometimes panic when our loved ones doubt God or choose to look for Him elsewhere than where we think He is or should be found. Everyone's faith journey is as different as their individual uniqueness. Just because someone has great doubts about God doesn't mean that's the way they will always think. Many times, faith is more of an evolution than a tangible fact. Allow someone to safely speak their present God-reality thoughts and feelings, whatever those may be. Then allow God's grace to work in ways your words can't. Your unconditional love speaks volumes in times like these.

CHAPTER 15

"Don't Fence Me In"
(Faith Returns)

Jenson wasn't cuddly as a baby, so it was a surprise and a delight when he did a 360-degree turn at age three and actually wanted to snuggle and be held—a lot. He would consistently remain my most affectionate and demonstrative child right up to his death. He wasn't afraid to hug his friends or family members and tell them he loved them in front of other people. Nor was he concerned about what anyone else thought when he displayed affection to Brian and me, even in his teen years.

Of my three children, he was also the one who gifted me with the most prolific number of notes and pictures, often signing them with "Your JEM." I treasure every jot and tittle he wrote and every picture he drew for me; they're all reminders of the love that was hardwired into his DNA. If love could've kept Jenson alive, both his for others and theirs for him, he would still be living, breathing, and walking on this earth. The fact remains, Jenson loved well and was well loved.

Not only did I love Jenson well, but I loved God well for all my late teen and adult years, too. That is, until Jenson died, and then a theological shift began growing in my heart and thinking during the dark days of grief after the shock had worn off. I wasn't sure I loved God the way I once had, and I began calling His sovereignty and goodness into question. And as stated in the previous chapter, I wasn't telling Him anything He didn't already know was in my heart and mind.

Around that fifth-month mark after Jenson's suicide, I was so overwhelmed with a longing to have him physically back in my life, it was obvious my accusations of God and theological turmoil were directly related to the missing of my son. Sometimes I had wanted other people back who'd died, too, but they were old or sick or had succumbed to Alzheimer's and were better off in Heaven. There was no "he's gone, but" with Jenson's death because there wasn't anything wrong with him that made his Heaven-going easier. He was a healthy, whole, complete person before he died. His death delivered no relief from any apparent illness or degeneration daily pulling him closer to the grave. His death only brought anxiety, confusion, and turbulence.

I believe that fifth-month mark was when I really began to question the theological view of God's control over all things. I couldn't reconcile God allowing Jenson to take his life with the love and healing of Jesus's ministry on this earth. Jenson's suicide didn't look like Jesus. To say God took Jenson's life, or He didn't intervene because He had better plans for all of us, is an indictment I just couldn't make upon God. He is against evil, not behind it, and Jenson's suicide looked like evil to me.

If God and Jesus are truly father and son and it's true what Jesus tells us, that if we've seen Him we've seen the Father, too, then the taking of the life of a child for some specific reason doesn't look like Jesus. And if it doesn't look like Jesus, I just can't seem to believe it's from God, either.

Jesus is full of compassion. He came to heal and make whole—to give life, not take it away. In Isaiah 53:4 we're told He has "borne our grief and carried our sorrows." He promises redemption out of our loss and pain, no matter how long we have to wait to see it. And the reality is very possible we may not even see much of that redemption on this side of Heaven.

This paradigm shift in my theology began my tenuous search for what God's sovereignty really looks like. Does He control all things, or are there instances in which He allows us free will in our actions? Does He have any say over the evil that happens, or does the evil actually come from His hand? Can God truly be good if bad things happen, and what does good even look like? How can suicide possibly be from God when Satan is the one who looks like suicide?

I haven't come to any steadfast conclusions in this search of mine, but more importantly, I haven't walked away from God, either. I have, however, redefined some of what I believe and have come to accept I can live without specific truths in theology and still follow Jesus. Ray Pritchard seems to understand my thoughts with his admission: "The connection with God in faith makes an immeasurable difference in my life. I think what I believe is true; otherwise I would abandon my faith. What I've experienced doesn't prove God's existence to anyone else (it barely does for me some days), but it does keep holding onto me and moving me forward."[32]

It's easier for me to no longer go to the deep, dark doctrinal places that make me doubt God. As theologian and author Gregory Boyd encourages, I prefer to keep my eyes on the things the Bible says about Jesus. Greg also makes sense with his reasoning that if it doesn't look like Jesus, and it doesn't sound like Jesus, then we should assume it's not from Him.

Jesus came to bring life, not death. Jesus came to bring redemption, not condemnation. Jesus looks like what love is supposed to look like. Evil and the really bad things in life make no sense coming from the hand of Love and Grace, the hand of Jesus.

I still haven't reconciled Jenson's suicide with any particular theological view, though. I'm at peace with holding on to Jesus while letting go of the "whys" of a suicide death. If I was supposed to know I assume I would, as, again, I don't think God is some big secret-keeper whom we're supposed to harass into telling us "why" things happen. Harassment and God don't seem to work conjointly.

Although I don't believe Jenson's suicide was an "oops" moment for God, either, I assume if there's a truth I'm intended to know in all of this, Jesus will reveal it to me. Perhaps it's kinder I don't know the truth, since the truth might just bring more guilt and despair. Sometimes, knowing truth is more painful than not knowing it. Besides, the truth won't bring Jenson back.

As time passes, I'm learning to rest more in waiting for redemption rather than striving for assuredness of alleged theological truths. I'm able to make assumptions from things I read, like Gregory Boyd's *Is God to Blame?* or Roger Olson's *Questions to All Your Answers*, books I highly recommend for those struggling with their faith.

One of the assumptions I've learned to rest in is that since God is fully revealed in Jesus, then everything that isn't consistent with Him is most likely not God's doing. Jenson's suicide isn't consistent with Jesus, so, therefore, if his suicide could have been supernaturally prevented, then I have every reason to assume it would have been. Why it wasn't, I don't know—and will it even matter when I get to Heaven?

I've also come to the conclusion that while living on this messed-up planet it makes far more sense to say that God is in charge, rather than that He's in control. I think we really need to be careful not to make all-encompassing statements about what God does or doesn't do. It seems there are many things that happen in this world that grieve Him and are against His will. Perhaps He truly does give us far more freedom and choices than some are prepared to accept.

I'm fully aware, however, that with my present view of God's sovereignty, I open myself up for criticism and judgment from some theological persuasions. But I can live with that, because my story and my journey are about God and me, not about God and those who find my theology questionable.

Kent Annan seems to speak my thoughts with his own words of, "May doubt win where it is true. Likewise may faith win where there is something real to trust. And may that faith be: That God's love is stronger than suffering. That God's love is stronger than death. That the unredeemable suffering all around will somehow be redeemed."[33]

Again, I wish the things I've learned since Jenson's death could have been discovered in a different way than through losing a child. Along with my frequent desire for a parenting "do-over" is also my wish for a faith "do-over" so as to find a less painful way of realizing the extent of God's grace and mercy. I can't say the things I've learned are worth the cost of losing Jenson, because I don't believe they are. I don't view his death as part of God's undisclosed or mysterious plan to make me a better person or teach me things I couldn't have learned in a kinder, gentler way.

And although, at present, I belong to a denomination that sees all things as part of God's plan, so, therefore, God must have taken Jenson for a reason, I don't believe that. We aren't God, and we don't know what His plans are, apart from wanting us to have a relationship with Jesus. To try to make a hurting parent feel better by telling them their child's death is part of God's plan, or happened for a reason, is just plain wrong and borders on cruelty.

Author Angela Miller phrases similar thoughts this way: "Sometimes things happen for no logical reason at all. Saying 'everything happens for a reason' is possibly the fastest way to make a grieving parent's blood boil. There is no reason good enough in all of heaven and earth that my son is buried underground while my feet continue to walk the earth. I get that most people say this in an attempt to make sense of what is senseless, but instead let's just state what is true: it makes no *bleepin* sense at all. Children should never, ever die before their parents."[34]

Statements about God's sovereignty or goodness don't typically offer comfort to a parent who is trying to understand why their beloved child died. Jesus didn't quote theology; He changed lives and comforted the brokenhearted with words of compassion and acts of love.

We have to be so careful not to worship theology in the way intended for worship of the Father, Son, and Holy Spirit alone. When our theology is more important than behaving like Jesus or being kind, we should really reevaluate what we believe. At times theology is important, but when we bring it into relational dialogue with someone who is hurting, we walk a fine line of offending where we should simply demonstrate love. In spite of what we may believe to be the only correct theology, none of us has the corner on truth.

This earth is a war zone, and we've lived in the nucleus of battle ever since Adam and Eve chose to eat from the Tree of the Knowledge of Good and Evil. According to Paul's words in Romans 8, this world, as we know it, groans in the bondage of decay. We're not promised an easy, pain-free journey in this earthly portion of our lives. If someone says otherwise, they're grossly mistaken. Jesus wouldn't have had to tell us in John 16:33b, "In this world you will have trouble. But take heart! I have overcome the world," if a trial-free life had been a guarantee.

We live in a fallen, broken world turned upside down by sin, and we have to live through each and every day on this messed-up earth until we go home to Jesus. As we live out our days we're going to be wounded and have our hearts broken and struggle with all kinds of hard things and suffer the loss of people we love. We're going to go through difficult times and get hurt and shed tears of deep grief and sorrow. This earth, as it is now, isn't our home and shouldn't feel as if it is. Our home lies beyond this fractured world.

There are very few guarantees in this life, and yet, other believers expect those of us who walk by faith to live as if there are. We're told what we're supposed to do, how we're supposed to behave, where our money is supposed to go, how we're supposed to dress, whom we're supposed to follow politically, whom we're not supposed to hang out with, and more. We have so many rules for living life we forget what freedom and grace look like. And then, because we can't measure up to all those rules, we ignore them but pretend we aren't.

No wonder people think Christians are hypocrites; in so many ways we are. We're far too often the only ones blind to the ridiculous legalism that chokes every ounce of grace out of our relationship with Jesus. Life with God was never supposed to look like a list of dos and don'ts. Life with God is supposed to look like grace, and grace is supposed to look like freedom. There is no freedom in being overstrung.

I wish I could tell you my faith has been unwavering each and every day since Jenson died. I wish I was one of those suicide-survivor mothers who continuously go to the scriptures in order to lift praises to God even in the midst of such great tragedy. Some people love stories like that and sing praises to such faith-filled hearts. I suppose some would prefer me to be a woman who was so connected to the Lord I could tell you I see all things, the good, the bad, and the ugly, as from the hand of God.

I guess it would be to my credit if people looked at me and could praise me for being pious or spiritual or unshakable or holy or devout or any number of words that make my faith more acceptable to what others think it should be or want it to look like—the stuff of historical saints' biographies we give to children and say, "Live like this." But I'm not that woman, and my guess is there are far more people like I am than those we write about in epic biographies of unshakable faith.

I promised myself, from the moment I picked my body up off the floor after learning Jenson had taken his life, I'd be completely honest about how he died and what I was feeling and thinking. To the best I know, I've told the truth about all of it. But if someone is looking for the story of a spiritual warrior who has conquered and won, that's not the tale I'm telling of myself. I have floundered and doubted and questioned and struggled and yelled at God and a whole host of other things that have not always demonstrated a strong faith. But I'm still here, walking with Jesus because I can't live without Him.

I'm also fully confident that just because I haven't lived out my grief as Christendom's definition of an unflappable spiritual champion, I'm not an embarrassment to Him, either. I don't believe He's disappointed in me, not even one little bit. Why would He be? Jesus loves Jenson even more than I do, so He's fully aware of what I've lost in this life. Losing Jenson wasn't His choice, either.

My story is still being written, one step at a time, and although Heaven will be my ultimate ending, I don't know about the conquering and winning here on earth. I take it moment by moment while my heart desires the same thing William Ritter asked of God: "I am not asking you to light up my sky, O Lord. Just find some way to keep my world from becoming terminal."[35]

Something to Consider: Just because someone redefines certain aspects of their theological beliefs doesn't mean they've walked away from Jesus. Just because they've left one church to attend another doesn't mean they're a heretic according to the exited church's denominational doctrine. There are many different denominations in Christendom, and they often hold to a variety of biblical tenets.

The bottom line is that we all need a relationship with Jesus, but after that, there seems to be a goodly amount of freedom in interpretation of specific teachings. As I often say in regard to legalism, very few things in life are completely black-and-white; there is a lot of gray, and that gray looks a lot like Jesus. Let's allow for a great deal of grace in the gray, especially if that's the place where Jesus hangs out most frequently!

CHAPTER 16

"Waitin' for the Light to Shine" (I've Changed)

In early December, the month after his tenth birthday, Jenson flew through the air after a huge trampoline jump and badly fractured his left elbow when he and the ground made contact. My poor son had to wait over nine hours in the ER before a doctor was available to set that elbow. It was well into evening darkness when that doctor came out to tell me how the surgery went. He ended our conversation with: "Your son is totally delightful and a bright light in a very dark place. I don't see children like that in my daily work here." That was my Jenson, a light in the darkness, even at age ten.

Because that light has been extinguished, my world is dimmer now, less bright than it once was. Although I'm so very grateful for the loved ones whom I still have on this earth, I'm simultaneously extremely sad and heartbroken because of that one who is no longer with me. I've been robbed of the delight of Jenson's presence.

There's now an empty place at the once-full family table reminding us of our loss on every holiday and at every family gathering. There's now one less stocking to hang at Christmas, one less family member to enjoy gift giving and opening, one less person to eat the leftover turkey after Thanksgiving, and one less loved one to enjoy Valentine's and Easter candy. There's one less person telling me he loves me when I need to feel loved and one less treasure to smile at me across a crowded room or when I walk through the front door upon arriving home.

There's a Portuguese word, *saudade*, which means the longing for someone or something that is loved but lost. It's a deep emotional state of nostalgic or profound melancholic longing for an absent person, place, or item so greatly loved— that overwhelming love remaining after someone is gone.

We pragmatic speakers of English as our first language don't have a similar word for *saudade*. Perhaps it's because we English-speakers don't do grief well, especially in the evangelical church. My heart is filled with such great *saudade* for Jenson, and yet it seems most people expect me to be fine, not the least bit crippled by the great love left behind from Jenson's absence.

Why are we expected to be "fine" after a brief time of sorrow? For a very long time I was not "fine" on a regular basis, and there are still those days when "fine" is not a qualifying word I would use to describe myself. I actually dislike that word, anyway, and prefer not to use it to label much of anything, especially since Jenson's death. It's such a noncommittal, nonemotional term. We "I'm fine" ourselves into a slow death of passionless dishonesty and lack of transparency!

About three and a half years after Jenson's suicide, I was visiting with a relative who is close to my age. Her children played with Jenson and Kalina during long Adirondack summers when they were all in their youth. Jenson was often the entertainment glue that kept them tied together in various activities. He always played that part well and was loved for it.

On this particular visit, after chatting for a while, I was told I seemed more like my old self. My relative meant no harm, but why did she have to say that? Sadness wrapped me in its covering as I later pondered her words and realized many people probably wanted me to be more like my "old self," the self I was before Jenson's suicide. They were comfortable with that "old self" of mine because that person didn't remind them of the death and loss that make people uneasy or distressed.

Since people typically dislike dealing with sadness and grief, if I was more like who I used to be, before my heart was ripped out and my world torn asunder, then this relative would have liked that better because she'd know what to do with me like she used to. But suicide had stolen my "old self," and I was now living part of my life untenanted with one of my treasures no longer next to me when I gathered my children close.

The "new me" is far more forthright and not nearly as upbeat or bubbly, so I may well have made my relative uncomfortable. I so wish she had said I seemed more peaceful or resolved or accepting or anything other than that I seemed like my "old self."

Those of us who've lost someone or something we love should be allowed *saudade* for as long as necessary. There should be no end of our loss, for loss has no end when someone has died and left us without their physical attendance on this side of Heaven. Why would anyone expect me to be like I used to be? I'm now filled with *saudade* for a missing, beloved son. A picture doesn't suffice when a presence is what's so greatly desired.

To propose I'm returning to my "old self" seems to suggest, at least to me, I'm over my grief, or have moved on to new things, or have forgotten how painful Jenson's absence is, or any other number of reasons we concoct so as not to look death in the face and call it what it is: an abhorrence to God's original intent for mankind. It's taken me a long time to realize that if my change in personality or behavior makes others uneasy, it's their concern, not mine.

Never being my "old self" again doesn't mean my "new self" has any less to offer those who prefer me unchanged. I'm allowed to be who I am now that Jenson is dead. I can't go back to who I was before he died. That's not an option, so I'm granted license to make the choice as to how I'll be in my "new normal." My nearest and dearest who share daily life with me have permission to speak about my "new" or "old" self, but others don't. I want to extend grace to those who mention how I've changed, but I would like reciprocal grace for who I am now.

Basically, I think I'm still the core person I was before my sweet son died. However, devastating loss, compounded with dealing with people over time, has most certainly redefined particular things about me. In some ways I'm even more sensitive than I used to be, but in other ways I'm more impenetrable, harder, and far more realistic. Although I've always been a crier, my tears often come more easily now, both in sorrow and in joy. And yet there are other times when even I'm confounded at how hard my heart seems on certain issues.

My extreme concern for what other people think of me has evaporated into my brokenness, and I shock myself with my own lack of caring as to people's perceptions of my words and actions. Along with that, I've become more cynical about the neediness of some, as I realize how many times I've allowed myself to be manipulated by the desires of others.

It's actually very freeing to give up the burden of caring what other people think. It's so sad, though, that grief and sorrow are the causes of this newfound freedom. I wish I could've changed without losing Jenson, but as L. B. Cowman states in *Streams in the Desert*, "It takes sorrow to expand and deepen the soul."[36]

When I'm weighed down with sorrow, it's not that Jenson went home to Heaven that makes me so unbearably sad and causes the most pain; it's the way he went home. Suicide changes the playing field of the anguish of a death, so of course I'm not the same person I was before Jenson's suicide. I'm not even the same person I was a year or two after he left. Tragic death has not only changed me but continues to do so as my life moves forward. Jerry Sittser describes it this way: "Catastrophic loss by definition precludes recovery. It will transform us or destroy us, but it will never leave us the same."[37]

Some of the ways I've changed are good. However, I'm not the same sweet, compliant person I was before. Even Brian says I'm edgier and challenge people and ideas much more than I used to. That's true. It's called survival and reevaluating my immediate environment and the world at large. It's called "I don't like the way a good chunk of life is, so what am I going to do about it?" It's called "finding my voice," and then using it to ask questions or make statements I was once afraid to speak or own because of what people might think. My present reality is that I don't much care what people think about me anymore. Freedom has come to me through loss.

In December of 2014, I wrote this to Tyler: "From my own experience, dear son, it is truly so very hard when the reality of life and the reality of ourselves are vastly different from what we thought it or we would be. However, there is a sense of freedom in letting go of what we thought we knew in order to find out what it is we actually need to know. It is hard work and at times more painful than we think we can bear but changes our perspective in a way that allows us to walk in grace for ourselves and the people around us." I can't go back, so the only way is ahead and forward.

There are some lingering anxiety issues from Jenson's suicide I never had before he died. Although I regularly got nervous at auditions and when performing, I was never particularly much of a worrier or riddled with anxiety. Now, however, I sometimes deal with what Brian and I label as "residual panic." This is a feeling that's often just below the surface of daily living resulting from sojourning through the reality of a loved one's unsuspected and totally out-of-the-blue suicide.

It's an ever-present apprehension sitting dormant until a situation reminds us of a past event revolving around Jenson's death. It's a thought that, when awakened, attempts to consume us if we listen to its whisperings for too long. Although it's not a conscious worry or uneasiness, when it happens it brings a memory flood of the same feelings that accompanied the experience of Jenson's suicide.

An example would be the night I attended an Advent service at a local college. I'd told Brian where I was, but he thought I was at a different location. When I failed to show up where he expected I'd be, he texted me, "Where are you?"

It was an hour later when I read the text and thought, "Brian never asks me where I am when I've told him where I'm going. There must be something wrong. What could possibly be wrong? Oh dear Lord, Kalina? Tyler?" and my mind took off in a whirlwind as I thought of the phone call from Brian when he needed me home to tell me Jenson was dead.

All those feelings of memory panic consumed my brain as I called him to find out what was wrong. In actuality, there was nothing wrong, whatsoever. He actually had forgotten where I said I was going, and a simple miscommunication had caused latent, residual panic to rise to a fevered pitch in my questioning brain. These happenings don't occur often, but when they do, it's almost impossible to rein in my emotions and think clearly at that particular moment.

Attending funerals has also become difficult since the end of 2011. Some are survivable; some are just too painful for attendance. I understand it's important for people to support the grieving family members left behind after a death.

Although I was so thankful for those who attended Jenson's memorial service, I also understood when, after the fact, people told me they just couldn't come because it was too difficult for them. Therefore, when funerals have arisen since death dealt a massive injustice to my own family, I'm hoping if I don't attend it's not viewed as a lack of caring, for it's never that.

Another way I've changed is how I think about the last words I speak to someone before I leave, go to bed, or end a phone or text conversation. I know Brian was racked with guilt for many months after Jenson's suicide. He felt his impatience and harshness were part of the reason Jenson took his life. Brian has great remorse he didn't stop home during the late morning of December 23 in order to speak to Jenson and apologize for his discordant tongue and behavior from the night before.

Several times over these past years since we lost our son, Brian has said we need to be careful of the last words we speak before saying goodbye or leaving someone. How true that utterance is in Brian's own life due to his initial perceived reasons for Jenson's suicide choice. Although he and I still fail at times, we try to leave each other, our children, and others whom we love without biting words if we're angry or upset with that person.

When we, or someone we love, close the door of a house or car and walk away, we don't know if we'll ever see that person again. If a relationship is strained, I usually hear that inner voice telling me to go back and apologize or try to make things right. The last words we speak to someone may haunt us forever if they're not spoken out of love and compassion.

It's grace that whispers, "Make this right, even if you don't think you're in the wrong." Is it better to be right or to suck up an apparent injustice and reach out in the love that bespeaks the value of a relationship? The answer to this seems blatantly apparent.

Something to Consider: Grief changes people; how can it not? We need to allow grief to make the necessary changes for the survival of those whom we know and love. It doesn't really matter if we like the "before person" better than the "after person." We can't go back; we can't even stay where we are; we can only move forward. It's the same for the person who suffers loss—going back or staying the same really aren't options.

I know change is disconcerting for many. Comfort and complacency are usually the easiest avenues and take the least amount of effort. Please remember any effort you put into accepting the changes in someone is minimal compared to the effort they've put into getting to where they are.

Grief is an achingly difficult path to walk. Don't make that path harder for someone by suggesting you like the "old" them better. That chapter has already ended. And don't suggest you like the "new" them better, either, because that may unwittingly add credence in their mind to any perceived culpability in their loved one's death. As my dear husband states, "Allow those who grieve grace to move within the walls."

CHAPTER 17

"Shall I Tell You What I Think of You?" (Opinions)

Well, perhaps I won't tell you what I think of you personally, but I will tell you I very much dislike hearing your opinions and wish you would keep them to yourself. Jenson didn't like hearing the opinions of others either. As a matter of fact, I think he hated hearing them more than I do.

He was my only child who regularly called me out on my behavior if he didn't like it, though, and he was usually correct in doing so. In hindsight, I appreciate his nerve with me; my peacemaking child was willing to speak up if needed.

It's not surprising he challenged my demeanor at times. He was so uncomfortable with angst and disagreements he would ask me why I was obviously upset when my anxiousness made him feel anxious. When I was impatient, he would let me know it bothered him. My sadness brought him down, and my intolerance was most frustrating to him.

Jenson could read me like a book, and when my behavior needed to be rewritten, he was the one to tell me how the words should go. However, he never sounded angry or disrespectful when calling me out on my conduct or tone of voice.

There's a song by Zach Williams titled "Fear Is a Liar," and although that's true, I think "shame" is also a bold-faced and bigger liar. Shame demoralizes us and tells us there's something wrong with who we are. It reeks of failure, defeat, insufficiency, and lack of acceptance. It tells us we aren't good enough, we can't do anything right, and we should, therefore, give up and rot away in our own disgrace and humiliation.

Opinions far too frequently rain down shame instead of encouragement, and, therefore, drop the receiver of the unsolicited words into a deeper muck of self-degradation. For several years after Jenson's suicide it was easy for me to go to a place of guilt and shame; I certainly didn't need the unsolicited opinions of other people to transport me to either of those feelings.

There are some opinions that are truly given out of a desire to help. I get that. The thing is, though, they aren't usually helpful even when uttered out of a wish to bestow sympathy or consolation. Brian and I were discussing this, and he explained it so well by saying, "Opinions are often given by someone who thinks they have a secret that will solve your problem or heal your wound, but they don't have empathy or context, so their words have no practical benefit even if given in kindness."

If we're trying to sympathize or empathize with someone, we should keep our opinions to ourselves unless someone asks us what we think. In circumstances of great suffering, we need to weigh every word we speak if we're truly going to be allowed the trust of sharing in the pain of another person. Our words must be filtered if we hope to be of any benefit to the brokenhearted. Opinions seldom evidence filtering.

Before Jenson died I didn't much like hearing people's unsolicited opinions; now I mostly find them intolerable and toxic. In general, however, many people love to share what they think. We often even label it "giving" an opinion, which I'll never understand since the word "giving" evokes generosity, and opinions are seldom magnanimous.

Rarely does anyone ask to share their opinion; it's just verbalized without much regard for the emotional state or circumstances of the recipient. My guess is, in situations like death, opinions are frequently shared out of people's discomfort and lack of knowing what to say. But as much as I understood the discomfort of others when they learned of Jenson's suicide, in the first several years after he died, it was excruciatingly difficult to listen to most of the unbidden words of unrequested opinions.

Sharing an opinion makes it about the person speaking rather than about the person listening. Sharing an uninvited opinion declares, "What I have to say is more important than how my words make you feel." Most of the time, I resent people giving me their opinion if I haven't asked for it, whether in regard to Jenson's suicide or anything else in life.

There was the man in a writing class who, after I read something I'd written about Jenson, told me I need to remember they all have problems and sad stories. But the way he said it made me uncomfortable. It didn't sound as if it was coming from a place of consolation. His eyes weren't kind, and there was no smile on his face. Did he mean I shouldn't speak about my dead son? Did he mean I made the class feel uneasy with my words, so "please don't do that again"? Perhaps I should have asked what he meant, but I didn't and instead just gazed perplexedly after him as he turned and walked away without giving me an opportunity to respond.

There was the pastor across the street from our house who told my hurting husband other people have it worse than he does. Really—he didn't think Brian already knew that? Wow, way to comfort my husband less than a year after our son died. Do pastors not receive any seminary training on how to be compassionate? Maybe "Compassion Role-Playing 101" should be a prerequisite class for anyone entering ministry.

Similar stories go hand in hand with these, and none of the people who shared their opinions made either Brian or me feel any better with their words. I doubt any of these people meant to be unkind, but when they shared their unwelcome opinion that was how they came across, in spite of their intentions. It was almost as if they were telling us, "Shame on you for not pulling yourself up by your bootstraps and getting on with life," to which my response would be "What?"—"How?"—and "Care to rephrase that?"

We all need to think and act more like Jesus. He wasn't an opinion-giver. He was a storyteller, a question-asker, and a listener. His means of communicating offers comfort and compassion to broken hearts.

"Let your conversation be always full of grace," says Colossians 4:6. It doesn't seem that unsolicited opinions fall under this definition, so please think about keeping them to yourself. Besides . . . if I really want to know what you think about something, I'll ask.

Something to Consider: Let's all remember the words of Paulo Coelho, who tells us, "The world is changed by your example, not your opinion."[38]

CHAPTER 18

"Oh, the Thinks You Can Think"
(Books)

Whenever given a choice of what to do on his birthday, Jenson almost always picked a day trip to a used bookstore somewhere within driving distance of a few hours. So it was no surprise when he chose to visit Tyler in Cortland and go to as many used bookstores as possible in Ithaca for his eighteenth birthday. Used bookstores were his favorite haunts, and Tyler was most likely his favorite person with whom to spend time.

Jenson was always reading some sort of book. His Christmas lists regularly included the titles of many filmmaking and animation manuals he desired to add to his collection, as well as an assortment of other books he wanted. Needless to say, reading was an important cornerstone of his imagination and artistic endeavors. That love of books makes a mother's heart proud, considering all the hours that mother spent reading to her children in their younger years. Books have always been extremely important to our family.

I don't remember all the details of the winter of 2012 other than directing *Seussical*, regularly going to counseling, rehearsing for *Fiddler*, and being constantly concerned about Kalina, Tyler, and Brian. And not only did I feel responsible for my own family's well-being but I also felt as if I carried the weight of everyone else struggling with Jenson's death—his friends, my friends, his girlfriend, her parents, the *Seussical* teens, and more.

What I do remember, though, is because I was being depleted and walking an unknown and unclear road of mourning, I began reading every book I could get my hands on related to suicide or the tragic death of a family member. Most of the books were about losing a child, and all of them were about losing a loved one in a traumatic way. Friends gave me books, I looked up books online, and I found books on grief and loss sites. As soon as I finished one book, I would begin another.

Books were my lifeline during the first year or two after Jenson's death. I'll always be grateful for specific ones I found and others given to me, or us, by dear friends who loved us very much. It seemed as if there was no period of free time during the months after Jenson's suicide that there wasn't a book in my hand providing words that proved beneficial to my heart and mind when I had a moment to sit and read.

I read a book written by a mother whose daughter ended her life the same way Jenson did. I read a book written by a man who lost his wife, daughter, and mother in one single car accident. I read a book by a father whose son fell to his death while hiking in Switzerland. I read memoirs, nonfiction, and suicide-survivor-help books.

For the most part, these books were extremely valuable and gave me much comfort and solace during the first couple of years, and, more specifically, the earlier months of my grief journey. There are specific titles I continue to purchase today and give to suicide survivors I meet. I have an entire tote of books that have siphoned the oil of healing into my aching mother's heart.

In addition to books, I scoured the internet for every blog or article I could find that addressed similar circumstances involving suicide. It's quite amazing how many titles pop up on the computer when a person googles "suicide survivor," or anything that sounds similar to that topic. Thoughtful friends also sent us links, too, and for those I was extremely grateful. It was as if I couldn't stop reading stories of others who had walked my similar path. Much of what I read online is still in a computer folder titled "Jenson," and I'm now sending these articles to other parents who are on the same grief journey.

Sometimes, though, I was given books or articles that weren't so helpful and frustrated me in one way or another. These writings, especially the ones written by prominent members of the "prosperity gospel or theology" culture, often seemed trite about loss and flippant about recovery. The authors made grief sound like an easy process if I just read their words or looked up their scripture-verse suggestions. After reading any of these specific writings I was supposed to be better, but I wasn't. I just ended up carrying more guilt and shame for not being so.

Still other books given to me had some good points but seemed to change the narrative of what was factual. One such book was written by a prominent member of the Southern Baptist Convention, a father who lost a daughter to suicide when she was in her thirties or forties. This father, and his wife, had struggled with the daughter and her issues since she was an adolescent. Their story wasn't similar to mine, but I read the book anyway because it was given to me by my kind and loving summer pastor, and I appreciated his thoughtfulness and generosity.

The father who wrote this book was kind in his writing but seemed to be attempting to redeem his daughter's reputation.

Perhaps he was; I don't want to judge the pain of another suicide-surviving parent. Each of us does what needs to be done in order to find our way through the horror-labyrinth of our child's death by their own hand. God knows this is a long and complicated journey.

At one point, the father wrote that if any of us had lost someone to suicide, a mixture of drugs and depression was involved in the death. This simply isn't true. Of all the suicide deaths of which I'm aware, and there are many, I know of only one that may have possibly been related to drugs, and that's not even a surety. Yes, depression is far too often involved in a suicide, but to say that drugs are, too, shouldn't be touted as truth.

This father continued to write his personal opinion about prescription drugs; he does not advocate their use. I understand his daughter had a drug problem, but that doesn't mean everyone who is depressed and on prescription drugs for their mental-health well-being is a potential suicide candidate because of those drugs. I dare say, of all those of whom I'm aware who took their lives, there may well have been multiple reasons for their deadly decision. We have to be careful not to assume we know more than we do and then state it as fact. Too often narratives are mistaken for truth, and thus allowed the potential for leaving carnage in the wake of the story taking on a life of its own.

So there are books I'll continue to give in the wake of a child's death, especially a suicide death. There are others I'll keep for myself and not recommend to anyone. I'm glad I've read all I have, but in good conscience, I'll leave some books, those that have the potential for causing more distress, guilt, or shame, in my tote, unseen by the eyes of those sojourning in their sorrow.

Something to Consider: By all means, give books and articles to those who are grieving. Some people will immediately devour them, and others will set them aside to read at a later date, or not read them at all. Please don't ask the person if they've read the book you gave them, though. It makes us really uncomfortable if you expect an answer and we didn't read your gift book, or we started it and didn't like it, or we didn't like it at all after we finished it. We don't want to tell you it made us feel worse, or we lost it somewhere in our messy grief-pile of things we can't find because our brains aren't working. Be generous with book giving, but take no offense if your book isn't appreciated or even mentioned at a later date. Grace declares, "Here's a gift; what you do with it is up to you."

CHAPTER 19

"I Sing the Body Electric" (Performing)

I majored in music in college. Voice was my chosen instrument, and although I played flute, violin, and piano, too, piano was by far my weakest skill. Because of this, I knew that if, and when, I ever had children of my own, they would begin taking piano lessons before they were old enough to have an opinion about any choice they might have over such.

Thankfully, Brian was on board with my "our children must have piano lessons" insistence in a discussion before we were even married. Would I have married him if he didn't agree with this? Most likely, but he's a musician, too, so there was no discord about future instrumental lessons.

In addition to playing piano, Jenson also began violin in his later elementary years. Violin was his choice. His large hands were great on the piano but always appeared somewhat awkward on the violin. Not one to invest himself one hundred percent into anything he didn't really love, he eventually gave up both the piano and the violin in his late high school years.

Playing an instrument wasn't his thing, so practicing was never a priority.

His piano skills did come in handy, though, when he began accompanying Kalina and creating music for his movies. Neither his piano nor his violin lessons were a waste when it came to his creativity with background sounds and songs in his films. I'm glad Brian and I insisted on instrumental lessons, but I'm also glad we didn't force their continuation when interest waned after many years of study and practicing.

Music often speaks to my soul in a way the Bible and other people don't, offering me the redemption of sound and beauty on an almost daily basis. I'm a singer of words and melodies, and these become the tools I use to artistically and creatively shape a song into my individual interpretation. I love the way phonemes and tunes reach into the depth of my being and convey legitimacy to the ache that cries out for comfort and validation.

My heart beats and my body moves to rhythms; my brain hums an unending array of melodic themes; and my soul interprets all the strains, airs, and pulsations into an ebb and flow of emotional cadences that sing out through my mouth and shine from my eyes, especially when performing. In my living of each day, I can no more fathom living without music than I can living without Jesus. Jesus and music are such defining entities of my daily existence.

My list of favorite songs grows ever longer as words take on a different meaning in light of Jenson's death. Words have always claimed my listening ear and reading mind, but now that demand has come close at times to looking like an addiction in my personal quest to relieve pain, explain reasons, and discover redemption. I go to songs for their salve over my soul as I would if ointment was needed on flesh; a grieving soul needs much to bolster it away from drowning toward the life buoy of healing.

Music is one of those saving life buoys for the healing of my heart and soul. It was why I needed to sing at Jenson's memorial service. I can still sing when I'm unable to speak. I can still sing when the spoken words of my own voice fail me.

In addition to music, certain aspects of the theater world have also afforded me redemption. Playing Fruma-Sarah in *Fiddler on the Roof* during the winter after Jenson died allowed me an escape from much of the encompassing sorrow filling our home and most of my relationships at that time. A year later, I was in *Sunday in the Park with George* at Schenectady Civic Playhouse. When I was still so broken inside, this was a healing time spent with past performing friends with whom I hadn't shared the stage in several years. They were as supportive and loving as the *Fiddler* cast the year before.

And the most redemptive role of all was playing Marmee in a production of *Little Women* about four years after Jenson's death. A few friends asked how I could do that role, since one of Marmee's daughters dies in the second act, but the reality for me was, how could I not? I needed to play that part as much as I needed to breathe at that time in my life. Moving out of myself into the character of another mother allowed me to leave my own grief while I lived hers, and that granted greater healing in my own hurting mother-heart.

It allowed me to think about how I wanted to realistically portray Marmee's pain in and after the death of her Beth. It allowed me to feel a death outside of my own circumstances so I could go back to mine and process lingering heartache. If I was believable as Marmee, I could continue to be believable as myself. The director gave me a huge amount of freedom to take Marmee's emotions wherever I felt they should go; for this I was most grateful.

I needed to sing Marmee's "Days of Plenty" out of my own mother's-heart loss. I needed to repeat the words to that song over and over until I could get through it and not break down.

I needed that challenge in order to move through more of my own inner sorrow. Jenson's best friend's sister, one of my past students I love, wrote me and told me how healing it was for her to watch me play Marmee. That role wasn't just for my own healing, but for others' as well.

Of all the characters I've played onstage, over all the years I've been in musicals, Marmee was the most curative part I've done. I was able to move on to more comedic and character roles after that, but it was *Little Women* I will always remember as a huge part of my restoration and redemption. It enlarged my aching heart so as to make it more tensile.

As much as I love performing, I now struggle with anxiety over being in front of people more than I did before Jenson's death. It seems I've lost a bit of my edge and gutsiness. I've always been hard on myself, expecting perfect performances or engagingly articulate messages when I speak. As hard as I try to relax with final presentations, though, I continuously second-guess my singing, acting, and speaking activities while my mind drones on with all kinds of criticisms about what I just did. Thankfully, I've learned this typically passes in a few days when resting relief wins over disappointment.

Lacking confidence and being substantially insecure in my performing has always been a legacy for me, to the point of making me wonder what I was thinking when I decided to become a singer and an actor. I cover well, though, and most who know or watch me would never guess my internal struggles.

I can hide behind everyone else when I'm directing a choir or a musical, but performing leaves me naked and vulnerable to either my own personal perceptions of my execution, or thoughts of what others might be thinking of such. This is one area where I still do actually care a bit too much about people's perceptions, in spite of what I said earlier. However, even as I admit this, I truly love performing when I'm able to lose myself in the giving of and bringing to life someone else's artistic and aesthetic creations.

But, owing to the suicide death of my son, the waves of uncertainty too often pull me under the tide of greater insecurity and cause my heart to palpitate at an alarmingly stressful rate. I think this is the parental legacy of a child's suicide. This type of death screams parental incompetence, ineptness, and blindness, so what does that say about everything else in our lives? If we couldn't prevent our child's death by his own hand, how can we capably and competently function with awareness in the world?

If we've so failed at one of the most important jobs to which we're called, why wouldn't we fail at everything else we're asked to do? This is an ongoing internal dilemma whenever I get up in front of people to audition, perform, or speak. I have a sense it may continue to be part of the carnage left over from Jenson's suicide, and, therefore, I'm not looking for it to go away as much as I'm working on battling it with mindfulness and grace.

The winter after Jenson died, a pastor friend gave us an article suggesting that rather than questioning and asking "why" something happened, we should instead ask, "What am I going to do with this?" and "To what purpose or end can this be used?" So that's what I went searching for—but not immediately; it took a few years for me to believe I had anything valuable to say to anyone.

Therefore, speaking opportunities have claimed more of my time in the last few years. Even though I'm often diffident with such, I count it a privilege to stand in front of others, mostly women, and share my story as a means of giving hope and encouragement.

It was important to actually survive for a few years after Jenson's suicide, though, in order to tell others how I was able to do so. It's never good to put a person in front of people so as to share their story and tout redemption until they've proven themselves trustworthy and believable. Why should anyone take to heart what I say if I'm not?

In her book *Sister*, A. Manette Ansay tells us faith is "The ability to believe. The ability to see beyond the place where you are."[39] If I was going to claim faith in Jesus, and share that faith, then I needed to believe in hindsight what I claimed as I spoke in front of others. I wanted to know it was true, and there were times I wasn't sure it was, as I was walking that daily grief path after Jenson's death. How wrong it would be for me to share something I neither believed nor lived.

I didn't want my story to be solely about me but about my Savior, too. Along with a very great amount of effort, purposeful hard work, resilience, time in nature, reading, searching, honesty, music, theater, and years, Jesus is a huge part of the reason I'm still here surviving, functioning well, and occasionally . . . even thriving. After Jenson died, I never thought "thriving" would be a word I could ever use to describe myself again, but sometimes I see it in me and realize how far I've come.

Something to Consider: When we are in the heart-wrenching early days of our grief, it's impossible to see or comprehend any possible future joy in our lives. We can't conceive how the activities that once brought us joy could ever bring us joy again. However, the reality may well be that joy is not something that comes to us by anything other than intention and mindful searching. It may actually be something for which we need to go looking. In grief, joy doesn't seem to just show up out of nowhere; we have to put forth effort to find it.

The activities I relished before Jenson died are the same activities that bring me joy in his absence. However, that joy is sometimes overshadowed by his lack of presence in the very thing I'm doing, especially if I'm doing something he may have done with me. But I do it anyway, because I'd rather think of

Jenson and know joy than simply not do something because it also brings a certain amount of pain. Many opposites go hand in hand no matter what the circumstances. Grace often shows up in the most ungracious places.

CHAPTER 20

"They All Laughed"
(Laughter)

At age twelve, Jenson was in his first production of the teen musicals I directed for twenty-two years. This musical was *Anne of Green Gables*, and he played one of the youngsters/schoolchildren in the show. At one point, the school students put on a historical tableau of life on Prince Edward Island—a show within the show. In this scene Jenson entered the stage as the required mountain of snow, clad in a full-length white crinoline tied around his neck and hanging down to his ankles.

Unexpectedly, that mountain of snow stole the audience's attention from the moment it stepped out from behind the back curtain. I should have warned the character who was speaking to wait for laughter at this point, but who would have expected such amusement from those watching? The mountain of snow took full advantage of the spotlight, and the face protruding above the crinoline lit up with delight at having captured the moment. By the sparkle in the eyes, it was obvious the wheels were turning as to how to milk this scene for all it was worth.

Applause began to ripple through the audience, encouraging more movement from the crinoline as it effortlessly swooshed downstage, spun around, and moved to its onstage spot among the rest of the cast. The original blocking was simple—walk on and move to your spot. However, that mountain of snow realized he had stolen the scene and seized the opportunity to command the stage. How could I reprimand the crinoline-wearer after the show? Comedy had staked its claim in a mountain of snow.

Two years later, at age fourteen, Jenson would go on to play Pigpen in *Snoopy!!!: The Musical*. He was adamant that he didn't want to do any solo singing, only spoken lines. But in one of the songs, it was a perfect spot for Pigpen to sing by himself in a large group number. However, "I don't want to sing a solo" was reiterated even more vehemently than the first couple of times it had been uttered.

The choreographer, not the director-mother, finally talked Pigpen into doing the solo with a lampshade on his head, since the line was about wearing said lampshade. This, of course, would be funny, and anything that brought laughter was agreeable to Jenson. A compromise was struck, and his voice loudly emanated from inside the lampshade while Pigpen took center stage.

Jenson loved laughter and making people cackle with joviality. He was quick-witted and bilingual in both humor and sarcasm. They were almost his first languages and flowed from his creativity with fluency and ease. He also responded with delight and greater gusto when he made people laugh, whether onstage in his teens or in his film and writing projects. Almost all of his animation was created to be funny. Comedy appeared to be his love language.

One of the ways our family functions is through laughter. We laugh at each other—at both the things we do and the jokes we make; we laugh at the people around us—yes, sometimes we make fun of you, and it lifts our spirits; we laugh watching Jenson's videos over and over again; we laugh at situations both ludicrous and unsolvable; we laugh at ourselves; we laugh as much as we can, and it feels really good to do so. I especially laugh loudly, with abandon and no care as to who hears me.

Brian and I were camping in Portland, Maine, a few summers ago. We love camping and exploring, and Brian is typically funnier when he's away from his office and we're out on the road. At the campground, he made jokes, used funny voices, and made fun of people passing our camper, and I laughed at all his antics. We were peaceful, safe, and comfortable away from our daily responsibilities, so I laughed a lot, and I laughed lustily. Sometimes we need a different life vantage point, so as to allow guttural laughter a chance to cleanse our grief-palates.

Of course, there's not much privacy at a public campground, so others could hear me laughing. As I was walking past the site across from us, that neighbor called me over to chat with her. She told me how good it was to hear me laughing and how much she enjoyed it. She said she doesn't hear people laughing much, and my laughter made her happy she was there. Is it really true we don't hear much laughter in our daily lives? Maybe I should take more notice of that.

She was camping alone, and I felt rather sad for her. I thanked her for her kind words and chatted with her briefly while petting her dog. I promptly went back to our camper and told Brian what this woman had said, ending my commentary to him by saying something along the lines of "If she only knew of our great tragedy and heartache, I wonder what she'd say about my laughter then?"

I often wonder about this in similar situations. None of the suicide-survivor books I read had any instructions about what to share or when to share. Perhaps in the first couple of grief years, when it's mostly about survival, there is no right or wrong answer to this conundrum. But Brian and I weren't camping in those first couple of years after Jenson's death. Now it seemed as if I should know what to do.

At moments like this conversation with our campground neighbor, I have a twinge of inner unrest that's hard to define. What do I share, and what don't I share, should the dialogue take a certain direction? How close do I let conversations get to my personal grief history? We weren't talking about family, so Jenson's suicide didn't need to be a topic for discussion.

This was a short, encouraging interchange where I was allowed to keep my tragedy to myself and not burden my neighbor or myself on a beautiful, sunny summer day. My laughter was encouraging to her, and that was all she and I needed to share with each other at a campsite where both Brian and I were enjoying a reprieve from the demands of daily life and the memories that so frequently haunt us.

The Bible tells us laughter is good for us, and we found this to be just as true in our early healing process as it is now. Good soul-laughter seems especially fitting for our Jenson-loss hearts considering how funny and entertaining he was. The winter after his death we spent much time watching comic and amusing sitcoms in the evening before sleep lay claim to our weary and wizened souls. These were a diversion from the burden of daily heartache, and the chemical reaction from our laughter momentarily eased our pain like the promises of a drug.

If it was funny, and I could find it at the library, we watched it. Jenson's girlfriend's family let us borrow a humorous sitcom we laughed our way through night after night, too. This evening ritual of humor became our diversion from the reality of no longer having our middle child.

I'm ever grateful for the gift of laughter, as it helped us survive during those long, dark nights of our doleful lives during the winter of 2012. It continues to help us survive as we walk the often disconcerting and tenuous years of daily living. Yes indeed, God is right about laughter being good medicine; I highly recommend it.

Something to Consider: Don't ever feel guilty about your laughter in the midst of your grief journey. You aren't being disloyal to the person who died. Laughter is a grace that allows us relief from our pain. Laugh often, and laugh a lot, even through your tears. Nowhere is it written you can't laugh and cry at the same time. Sometimes the only way we can get from our moment of where we are to our moment of where we need to be is by doing both in sync.

CHAPTER 21

"It Never Entered My Mind"
(Satan/Evil)

Sir Isaac Newton's third law states that for every action, there is an equal and opposite reaction. That statement means that in every interaction there is a pair of forces acting on the two interacting objects. In other words, forces result from interactions. I didn't think much about this law until I had children! Being a mother brought much truth, light, and experience to Newton's law of motion. Being a mother brings light to a lot of things.

Even though Jenson was a pleasant child a relieving portion of the time, he pushed the limits of dangerous and unacceptable exploits after he began walking and exploring. If there was anything to break, stick into a body cavity, fall into or off of, climb on, or unsafely eat, he was my child to do it. He was also the one to typically take things apart and, therefore, ruin a goodly number of usable objects. In light of all his kerfuffles, it's hard to believe he wasn't my most active or hyper child.

It was Jenson my sister found flailing facedown in her small pond after she turned her back for a matter of seconds when he was a toddler. He was the one who stuck a crayon up his nose that had to be removed with very long tweezers in the ER. He swallowed a watch battery, thus initiating daily poop checks until it was found. It was Jenson who set off the alarm at John Brown's Farm by opening a door that was clearly and obviously intended to stay closed. And he was the one who broke the arm off a statue at the Schenectady Museum when he climbed up on its pedestal and pulled it over. That repair claimed over one thousand dollars out of our bank account.

As homeschool parents, we were quite involved in the Patriarchal movement for several years. This was one of the heavy-duty controlling sectors of the conservative Christian homeschool campaign promising a great future for us and our offspring if we followed their specific tenets for behavior, attitudes, decision-making, and the raising of "Godly" children. These tenets included "the purity/modesty culture," courtship rather than dating, the early push for teens to become mature adults, debunking the idea of adolescence, demanding great responsibility at a young age, and more.

In my ponderings over reasons for Jenson's suicide, my thoughts used to jog to Patriarchy and that part of our homeschool life. In many regards, we believed the promises and guarantees assured to us and our children if we bought into this movement and mentality. It all made family life sound so wonderful compared to the dysfunction in which both Brian and I had been raised. Brian was such a conscientious father that he spent many hours training Jenson into what Patriarchy defined as "proper manhood."

In the earlier aftermath of Jenson's death, I wondered if all that emphasis on masculinity and maturity was just too much, too early for our precious and sensitive son who didn't fit into any designated mold. Did Jenson question the importance of accepting responsibility and growing into adult behavior and expectations before a person had matured mentally or emotionally? He often declared he didn't want to grow up. Did he feel too much pressure to do so?

Why did the leaders of the Patriarchal movement think they could redefine the immaturity and instability of the teen years into something psychology has experientially proven otherwise? The teen years are really hard and deserve understanding and patience. If they are tritely skipped through or not taken seriously, there are future consequences for the lack of freedom in proper development. Did Jenson feel as if he was expected to make decisions about his future he just wasn't ready to make? These were more unanswered questions.

Needless to say, the following of any aspect of the Patriarchal movement was not one of our better parenting choices. Thankfully, we didn't buy into the whole thing in total hook, line, and sinker fashion. But we were involved enough that once we stepped away from all that it espoused, I never, ever wanted anything, whatsoever, to do with Patriarchy, again. That word now raises huge and vivid red flags of concern in my mind if I ever hear someone using it to encourage specific teachings.

I share these things because I'm back to Newton's third law of opposites. In spite of the good that I see in the world, I now have a greater awareness of evil since Jenson's suicide. His behavior as a child, although not what would be considered wicked by any means, was sometimes dangerous and brought about reactions that were the opposite of peacefulness and patience. The Patriarchal movement had some good points, but it demanded too much parental control, was not grace-filled, and promised guarantees where there are none. We live in a world where we see both good things and very bad things on a daily basis. There is no escaping these opposites, no matter how fast and furiously we run to do so.

As I stated earlier, we live in a fallen, broken world that doesn't work right much of the time. When I stare into the face of Jenson's suicide death, I have a greater understanding of what evil and Satan look like. Satan came to kill and destroy. Satan came to steal and maim. Satan is the antithesis of Jesus, who will one day cast that evil wretch into oblivion. Until then, however, Satan works his evil here, and I think his lies took Jenson out. Suicide looks like Satan; it doesn't look like Jesus.

The summer after Jenson died, Brian began seeing the pastor of my grief counselor. He'd been meeting with our own pastor, but since that man didn't really understand the depth of our grief, my counselor suggested hers might be more helpful to my husband. As it so happened, he was a good fit for Brian, who I don't think would have worked through as much of his bereavement if it hadn't been for the wisdom and thoughtful counsel of this particular man.

Brian saw this pastor for a few months on his own, but then in late fall of 2012, I began joining them for some of their sessions. It was good for us to meet with someone together as a couple, too, since we were both continuing to grieve in somewhat different ways, and we'd stopped our time with our hospice counselor by then.

While at one of our counseling sessions, this pastor asked me, "Why do you keep saying Jenson killed himself?"

"Because he did," I responded. "Isn't that what suicide is, killing yourself? I want to always be honest about how Jenson died."

"Well, when we say someone killed himself, it implies he was in control of his mind and knew what he was doing," continued the pastor.

"Why would someone take their life if they weren't in control of what they were doing?" I asked.

He went on to explain, "It's often assumed that someone who takes their life isn't thinking as they normally would. The person believes a lie because their brain isn't processing truth correctly."

To that, I said, "I'm not sure I understand."

"What if Satan, or evil, if that sounds more believable, convinced Jenson to ignore the truth and believe lies about himself? Those lies convinced him he should take his life. The only real power evil has over us is deception, and Jenson was deceived. Satan is masterful at that," he explained.

I was trying to follow his train of thought, but I was also finding it rather disturbing. This was the first time I'd contemplated anything like this. I didn't really want to think of all the ramifications involved in Satan taking out my son, but it made more sense to me than Jenson choosing to kill himself when he was in his right mind.

I would see my own counselor soon after that meeting with her pastor and ask her if she thought he was a wacko. She didn't, and told me she had the same thoughts about Jenson's death. I like the way she phrased it, though, a bit differently than her pastor had. She said, "Jenson did not take his life; his life was taken from him."

I've never been one to walk around thinking all the bad things in life are due to Satan or demon activity. I don't assume "the devil made me do it," because I'm a firm believer in the strength and capacity of personal stupidity and, therefore, the reality of consequences and individual accountability. I'm not a person who follows every whim and fancy, especially those of a spiritual nature. Those who know me best might even call me a skeptic about many things I hear. I don't blindly believe or follow much of anything of a supernatural or divine disposition.

I'm typically the tiresome person asking questions; my hand is the one raised in the air seeking clarification while my children roll their eyes. I'm Thomas, the disciple asking to see the holes in the hands and side of Jesus before simply believing what he's told. I'm educated, intelligent, and well-read, so after my counselor spoke those words, it was huge for me to have a sense of peace I hadn't had since Jenson's death.

After that, I tried to never again say "Jenson killed himself." In my journal I wrote, "In the book of Job, the greatest mystery is that of undeserved suffering. Perhaps it is true Satan is behind Jenson's death more than any other reason."

Something changed in my spirit from that point on, and I stopped my internal, frenzied striving for reasons, answers, or explanations for Jenson's suicide. I did, however, continue looking for redemption, because as Max Lucado states so well when talking about Joseph, an Old Testament hero and Pharaoh's right-hand man in Egypt, "What Satan intends for evil, God redeems for good. 'You meant it for evil; God rewrote it.'"[40] I stopped my desperate search for motives and began resting in how God would rewrite the evil that robbed me of my son!

Something to Consider: Sometimes our frenzied searching is to no avail when looking for answers, as there just aren't answers we can find, see, or discern. Ephesians 6:12 tells us, "For our struggle is not against flesh and blood . . . but against the powers of this dark world and against the spiritual forces of evil in the heavenly realms."

I don't know how to explain evil other than it seems what we see is not all there is. Perhaps this is why I so appreciate the writings of C. S. Lewis, J. R. R. Tolkien, and Madeleine L'Engle. They weren't afraid to take on the unseen evil so evident in this world. And all of them also seemed sure of what I know to be true, too: that in the end, God will win.

CHAPTER 22

"In This Wide, Wide World" (Suicide Awareness)

When my three children were too young to be left home alone while Brian and I attended the annual NYS homeschool convention, my sister would graciously entertain them at her house while we were away. They loved going to their aunt's house, which included a creek and pond for unlimited water antics, endless other outdoor activities, garage sales to attend with money to spend donated by my sister, yummy edible treats not regularly enjoyed at home, wild critters to stalk and catch, and . . . GOATS.

Oh, how Jenson loved my sister's goats. She told me he was especially enchanted by the babies, and when he would disappear she would discover him perched on a ledge in the goat barn cuddling those adorable creatures. While his brother and sister were running around like wild maniacs, Jenson would spend hours lovingly interacting with little snuggly kids.

My sister made a trip to the barn to check on Jenson one afternoon when she couldn't find him. She couldn't contain her amusement when she came upon him with his little rear end wedged tightly into a water bucket, feet dangling a foot off the ground. A mother goat had butted him backward, and the amount of water in that Jenson-bottom-filled bucket anchored both pail and child to the ground. Help was required to get that little goat-lover out of his predicament.

Help is often required to get us out of predicaments. Sometimes we think we can manage on our own, but we don't know enough about situations to make intelligent decisions so we make assumptions instead. Assumptions aren't necessarily correct. Even experts in particular fields make assumptions, too, when they don't look or listen appropriately and astutely enough. When that happens, the help that's given isn't necessarily useful in the way it should be. We all need the ability to see the big picture and not get hung up on minutiae or statistics.

The fall before Jenson's eighteenth birthday was uneventful. He neither took classes nor worked full time. He spent time with friends, worked on his filmmaking and the book he was writing, and planned to begin online college full time in January.

As I look back on this season of his life, I see nothing out of the ordinary for him, no foretaste of the impending doom of his devastating decision that lay a few months down the road. He was almost always pleasant and buoyant, with no signs of unrest or melancholy. There appeared to be no hint of darkness in his life—at least nothing visible that would spark notice in friends or family. I really do believe it's hard for people who don't know us or Jenson to accept that we didn't see anything in his behavior that would give us cause for distress, to assume he was depressed, or to even contemplate the possibility of his suicide.

All the literature I've read from the American Foundation for Suicide Prevention, and the workshops I've attended with that same organization, state that 90 percent (or nine out of ten) of those contemplating the taking of their lives will give signs, say something, or demonstrate in some way that they're planning it. However, the facilitators of that organization never talk about the other 10 percent, and when I ask about that one person out of ten, they just stare at me. I don't think anyone I've spoken with who's involved in suicide prevention truly believes, in reality, that a suicide could just happen out of nowhere and blindside family and friends.

But . . . Jenson's girlfriend and her family saw nothing, his closest friends saw nothing, and we, his family with whom he lived, saw nothing. His suicide would be a shocking blow and rock the safe world of a great many people who knew him personally or through others.

Statistics say those who complete suicide due to a diagnosed or visible mental illness comprise 90 percent of those who take their lives. The stats also say, since that 90 percent will most likely give some sort of hint as to their intentions or cry out for help in some way or another, a suicide may be avoided with intervention and/or confrontation. Ninety percent is a very large number, but it's not a hundred! Ninety percent leaves 10 percent for whom no one can actually account as to why they choose to end their lives.

Suicide-prevention training sessions teach you how to talk to those who may be contemplating their own deaths. It's good to know how to do that, because the information on such has changed over the last several decades. We're finally able to openly dialogue about mental-health issues and suicide, something almost unheard of when I was Jenson's age.

The professionals involved in suicide awareness and prevention are good, compassionate, intelligent folks who want to bring these deaths to an end and who spend hours both in learning for themselves and training others so as to educate the population and bring awareness to suicide prevention. They do wonderful work in these areas.

When they look at me, though, and I tell them Jenson's story, I can see in their eyes and hear in their voices they don't believe my son was part of that 10 percent who give no clues as to their intentions toward death. I speculate they have to say there's 10 percent who show no signs of mental-health issues because there are the Jensons who take their lives, but I don't think they really believe someone dies that way without showing any signs of their intent.

When I share about Jenson, I think they assume all of us who knew him missed something he was actually trying to tell us. I don't know, maybe we did, but if so, why were all the people I know who were close to him totally taken by surprise with his decision? Could that many of us have been so completely clueless?

In the spring of the second year following his suicide, I attended a safeTALK training session offered by a prominent suicide-prevention organization. This organization does excellent work in raising awareness about suicide in hopes of seeing the numbers drop.

I went to this training session at the suggestion of my grief counselor when I was looking for ways to find redemption out of Jenson's death. I thought working against suicide might give me purpose, and my counselor knew of safeTALK; she'd gone to one of the sessions herself. Plus she was acquainted with the woman in charge, so she put me in contact with her.

In hindsight, it was too soon for me to go to something like that, but who knew—because I seemed to be doing well. I certainly don't blame my counselor for suggesting I take part in the seminar; I'm the one who brought up the topic and asked her. She even said, "Are you sure?" and I said, "Yes!"

The afternoon I attended that session ended up very messy and extremely unpleasant for me as I became unraveled by the facilitator and the others in the class. My unraveling wasn't precisely due to them, however, as much as to my own frailty at that time.

The safeTALK training was located in the basement of a building in a room with very low ceilings and no windows— strike one for me and a double whammy of unease. Being underground with low ceilings and no windows makes me feel claustrophobic. There were a lot of us in there, too, so we were rather tightly crammed at the tables. Even on good days, I'm not comfortable being tightly crammed anywhere; this was strike two.

We watched a film that taught us how to recognize the signs of someone contemplating suicide, as well as what kinds of questions to ask that person. The facilitator then opened up the room for discussion.

When people began asking questions and making comments it was my strike three, and I thought all their talk was going to put me right over my emotional edge. At one point, I even left the room and went to the women's bathroom, where I worked on trying to prevent myself from becoming a sobbing mess. After I calmed down and returned to the classroom, I continued struggling to hold myself together.

The other attendees weren't being thoughtless or unkind; they were just approaching the subject from a point most come from when they haven't had direct contact with a suicide. I know it was my perception of the "stupidity" of their comments and questions that caused me to finally speak out.

I think it was the woman who asked, "Isn't it against the law to commit suicide? Who gets charged with that?" that finally gave me the courage to raise my hand.

I reminded them there really are those who take their lives even if there appears to be no reason. I told them about Jenson and began crying, and they all just stared at me and said nothing. Why does the evidence of grief so often bring statue-like, stony behavior from others?

For what seemed like far too long, the room remained completely silent until the facilitator finally asked me if I was seeing a counselor and getting help. Yes indeed, he turned it back to me and didn't even address someone taking their life without obvious cause or visible intentions. At no point that afternoon was there any time, whatsoever, spent discussing the 10 percent of no account.

The woman with whom I originally signed up for the class, the one my grief counselor knew and who'd been in the room the entire time, didn't say one word to me when I thanked her for allowing me to participate at the end. She hardly made eye contact, only gave me a half smile, and uttered nothing at all.

When I shared details of my afternoon with my friend Kate, who is a social worker and counselor, she asked me why I go to things like that alone. That was a good question. I guess it was because I thought I could handle it, and I didn't want to be a burden to anyone by dragging them to something that might make them feel uncomfortable. The potential of being a burden to someone was far more distasteful to me than the possibility of any angst from a suicide awareness and prevention training session.

It would take me a good year after that before I attended anything similar again. For the time being, I stopped looking for redemption in that arena.

Something to Consider: In spite of what I've shared, I do truly believe suicide prevention and awareness organizations do great work. These are the people who help with organizing suicide-awareness walks, classes like safeTALK, training of professionals to go into schools in the aftermath of a suicide, survivor support groups, survivor remembrance days, suicide hotlines, and more. They are responsible for much of the change that is good and helpful in dialoguing about suicide. I'm extremely grateful for the work they do.

Brian invited the head of the Capital Region chapter of the American Foundation for Suicide Prevention to come speak at his Rotary club. She did an excellent job and brought information to light that is still not often openly discussed. Even when we know of a suicide, we don't always know how to tackle the topic. I highly recommend including talks on mental health and suicide awareness when planning organizational meetings. By arming people with knowledge, a life might be saved.

CHAPTER 23

"Climb Ev'ry Mountain" (Survival)

Water-skiing is one of my great life delights. Our summer-cabin neighbors got me up on skis when I was six years of age, and I've absolutely loved it for all my summers since then. Of course Brian and I taught our own three to water-ski when they were younger. It seemed a prerequisite for enjoyment at a lake abode. Two hated it, and one liked it; he still does. Jenson happened to be one of the two.

As determined as my middle and youngest were to not enjoy water-skiing, I was equally resolute that it was only possible for them to like it when they improved and were good enough to pop out of the water and circle our lake several times. Therefore, every time Brian, Tyler, and I skied, Jenson and Kalina were expected to try, too.

I did everything I could to help them get up and stay up—I got in the water with them, I gave instructions from the boat, I had them try different-length skis, I sat on the dock to see if starting from there was easier, I cheered, I scolded (never effective), and I promised they'd love it if they would only stick with it. Nothing I did helped much, at all, and enthusiasm waned.

It would be Brian who held the magic key to Jenson finally getting up and staying on top of the water for a good long ski; one day he offered to get in the water and help. I drove the boat and Kalina spotted. With Jenson's watery yell of "Okay," I increased our speed while continuously swiveling my head to alternate between watching my son and watching where I was driving. In one of my front-facing moments I heard Kalina yell, "Mom, Jenson lost his bathing suit."

Sure enough, Jenson was wearing nothing, but he was out of the water and skiing with a huge smile of utter delight plastered on his face at both his accomplishment and his nakedness. I headed out to the middle of the lake, where I hoped no one could see anything other than my son's tan line. I cheered with a mixture of enthusiasm, embarrassment, and hope that no one had their binoculars out. From the water behind us, Brian waved Jenson's bathing suit in the air like the flag of success it was at that moment while Jenson made it around the middle of the lake a few times before I headed toward shore and he let go near our dock.

Since naked water-skiing isn't particularly appreciated or accepted by anyone watching, Jenson's career for such was short-lived. His preference lay with tubing, where speed was the key and bathing suits were necessary for nonchafing survival. Sometimes it's survival that calls the shots.

After Jenson's death, I had to make the decision to continue on with directing *Seussical: The Musical* with the homeschool co-op teens or cancel the production. His girlfriend was to be the Cat in the Hat, and Kalina and his best friend were in it, too, as were many of his other friends, but I no longer had my Horton. If I carried on with the show, every rehearsal would be a reminder my sweet son was no longer living on this earth. I had to decide whether staying the course would be healing or just too difficult. Could I survive the whole process?

Many people kept telling me to do what was best for me, but the problem was I couldn't figure out what that was, because I was so used to doing what seemed best for everyone else. My people-pleasing nature didn't just automatically die with Jenson. I seemed incapable of weighing out the better choice for my own pain against what was best for the *Seussical* cast.

I love working with teens; they're some of my most favorite people in the world, and this cast was a delightful one. I couldn't only think about myself and what I'd have to endure. I wasn't able to separate myself from what would be encouraging to everyone else, nor could I imagine not directing the musical and disappointing the teens even if it was really hard for me to move forward with the show.

As I continued wrestling with some sort of decision, I realized I had to find someone to replace Jenson if I decided to proceed. That, of course, would be no easy task, considering how hard it had been to find a Horton in the first place. I was now at a loss as to who could possibly step in to play that part. A son can never be replaced, but a cast member can, even if it's wearisome to do so.

The name of one of my female graduates came to mind. I contacted her, and she enthusiastically agreed. Therefore, with a Horton in place, I decided it was best to continue, and rehearsals began before Jenson had even been dead for a month.

I'll always be grateful for the decision to follow through with that production. As emotionally difficult as it was for me at times, it would have been harder not to have the responsibility of the musical. It helped me survive by keeping me going for over four months, and I very strongly believe it was healing for the teens, too.

Because of twice-a-week rehearsals, they were able to spend a good amount of time with each other, enjoy a diversion from daily life that may have been depressing without Jenson, and communally grieve his loss when they didn't have the tools to do so independently. There was also a good amount of laughter and encouragement that went on during the months of working together. That seemed far healthier for fragile teens who may have otherwise been sitting home alone in tears pondering why someone they admired took his life.

When we're staring our grief in the face during those beginning days of the truth of our new reality taking form, we don't know what's best for our survival. Even though all of us will be touched by death during our lifetime, the suicide death of a child, parent, or loved one isn't something most people typically experience. It takes its toll in ways other deaths don't. Even with all the books I read, even with my faith in Jesus, even with all the support I had, I still had to do an immeasurable amount of figuring out how to survive the loss of Jenson in my life.

Survival isn't a one-size-fits-all commodity. Sometimes it's a fly-by-the-seat-of-your-pants dance that leaves you flat on the floor when your feet slip out from under you on the glossiness of cheap promises, from both others and your own brain. Sometimes it's a wrong turn, because one direction looks easier to navigate than the one that demands more work. Sometimes it's just listening to whichever voice speaks the loudest in your head at any particular moment. And sometimes it's found in the simple beauty of the things that consistently allowed you to survive life from day to day before death changed your future.

The Adirondack Mountains, my most favorite place in the world, were good medicine for the darkness of my questioning mind and the survival of my soul the summer after Jenson died. In the early days of that season I spent time alone at our cabin while Kalina was on a trip to the Netherlands. The weather was spectacular, a gift from God, even though I was so very angry with Him at that time.

During the long July days I would aimlessly drive back roads, and at night I would sit with my feet in the water at the end of our dock hurling allegations at God into incredibly bright starlit skies. I swam in the sun, hiked with our dog, and slept to the serenade of loon songs. I was surrounded by beauty wherever I went, and I soaked it in as the healing balm it was. The mountains and their beauty were my refuge. They continue as such in my life.

During one of my times at our summer cabin in 2012 I wrote, "I cry so hard at the beauty, which causes pain, which somehow soothes my soul. I don't understand the mystery of it, but I am thankful." I've come to realize how important beauty is to my survival. Sometimes I sit quietly while I rest in it, and other times I have to look for it like a body desperately needing its regular drug fix. It is beauty that often brings the soul-ache that then eases the heartache. It is beauty that also reminds me of God's love and grace.

Everyone wears daily-life survival in a vastly different fashion, and I've discovered the amount of love given someone doesn't guarantee their choice to stay when considering suicide. I've read books written by the parents of a child who chose to end his or her life, as well as listened to parents, in my own personal relationships with them, who've survived the suicide of one of their precious children, their one child unable to claim their own individual survival.

Each of these mothers and fathers unconditionally and devotedly loved the child of whom they wrote or spoke. Each was ravaged and razed by the suicide of that beloved child. And each has drudgingly toiled through the muck of the heart-wrenching and soul-mutilating carnage left in the aftermath of their child's choice to die rather than live. Most of these parents have survived, but some have been so shattered, their hearts ruptured and rent by the pain of their loss, they've followed their child out of this world by making the same choice to end their life.

I understand that despondency and despair, but what a tragedy for the family members left behind once again, a second suicide on the heels of the first one. I get the decision to leave, though, because our child's choice to exit from this earth seems like a direct affront to our parenting, love, and care for them. How is their choice ever equalized in light of the depth and extent of our own parent-heart's absolute love for the child we've birthed from our very flesh and blood?

Whenever I hear of or read about the suicide death of a son or daughter, I try to reach out to the mother of that child, another way I survive. I've met so many other parents walking their own suicide-survivor journeys, and when I offer encouragement by traveling with them through their grief and mourning, it brings me tangible redemption out of my own loss.

Not all choose relationship, but when they do, I consider it an honor to enter their pain and suffering. I truly understand the intensity of the carnage and know how difficult the journey is to some sort of functional healing. I really do "get it" and am willing to sit with them in the ashes of their brokenness.

Coming alongside suicide-survivor mothers isn't a drain on my personal empathy. I want to be there for them because I know the reality and depth of their pain. What parent would ever prepare for this death-departing choice their precious child makes? What parent comprehends all their child's suicide means to the rest of the days of their own lives or the lives of their other children? What parent can imagine life without a particular child in their family, no matter what that child deals with or suffers on this side of Heaven?

My own journey has opened doors into the hearts and lives of some very special mothers and fathers whom I love dearly and value greatly because of their inherent personal loss, honesty, and transparency as we walk the same road. Their questions, statements, doubts, and challenges don't cause me to cower in disregard before my own loss. My own loss doesn't hold sway over not entering the story of other survivors. I've learned the truth of what L. B. Cowman means when she tells us that each of us who suffers difficulty has a life that "becomes the hospital ward where you are taught the divine art of comfort."[41]

There is my dear friend Karen, whose twelve-year-old daughter, Lauren, took her life a year and a half before my Jenson. Lauren would have been thirteen three weeks after her death. She was a beautiful girl, kind and loving, showing no signs of depression or mental illness before her suicide. Breeanna Rose, another beautiful twelve-year-old, took her life the day after Christmas, and her mother, Mona, as with Karen, has never found out why her daughter made that choice.

I met Lorraine after I played Marmee in *Little Women*. Lorraine's forty-two-year-old son, Robert, had struggled with depression much of his life and finally made the choice to end it here and go to Heaven, leaving his mother devastated as she worked through her grief. Susan's forty-nine-year-old son took his life and left behind a wife and two young children. Susan's husband, who was not her son's father, wondered when she was going to be better and not cry so much. How can a mother ever stop crying for her dead child?

Debbie's son, Jonathan, age twenty, recommitted his heart to Jesus on Mother's Day of 2019 and then took his life the very next morning. When Debbie tells me about what Jonathan was like, I'm reminded of the same loving, compassionate, kind, and thoughtful ways of my Jenson. I met Russ and Yanna in Halifax, when they were only a year and a half from their twenty-four-year-old son's suicide. As I listened to them describe their Garret, I realized he was as creative, tender-hearted, intelligent, and kind as both Jonathan and Jenson.

I know Christine because of my husband's work with rescue missions and homeless shelters. Her thirteen-year-old,
Jeremy, took his life after a normal family dinner. Christine
found him dead the next morning when she went downstairs
to turn off his alarm. She tells me he was a peacemaker and
her thoughtful, considerate child. And there is Marie, whose
professional-athlete son took his life in Boston at age twenty-
four. Marie was not even a year from Jack's suicide when
COVID-19 hit and she had to deal with social distancing and
the residual isolation from that. At a time when she most
needed the bodily presence of others, she had to remain by
herself during the days when all the shock had worn off and
she had to figure out how to accept Jack not being a physical
part of her life again. Jack was Marie's kind and thoughtful son.

Why is it that these sensitive and gifted children seem so
susceptible to taking their own lives? What is it about death
that's more appealing to them than life? Are their lives so difficult here they choose to exit the messiness before God intends
to call them home? Should we therefore not tell our children
about how wonderful and beautiful Heaven is?

My counselor said Heaven looks like a better place to teens
who don't have the tools to cope with this present world or
see beyond the moment because of their impulsiveness. Does
that just make the choice to leave easier for them when making
their deadly decision? If so, it seems it's not only teens who
think this way and make this choice.

This is a horrible club in which all these mothers, fathers,
Brian, and I share membership, and although none of us made
the choice to join for ourselves, in some inexplicable way, it
helps to know we're not alone, and others walk the same road.
William Ritter tells all of us we are part of "the fellowship of
those who bear the mark of pain."[42] He's right, you know.

Whenever I first meet someone who has lost a child to suicide and share with them that I have, too, their sense of relief

is palpable. It's almost as if their entire body exhales a reprieve while their heart, soul, and mind silently whisper, "Thank you; finally, someone who really gets it."

In addition to reaching out to others walking the same suicide-survivor road, Brian wanted a more tangible way for us to bring something worthwhile out of Jenson's suicide. Therefore, his business partnered with Schenectady County Community College to start the Jenson E. Merriam Memorial Scholarship Fund. This is a scholarship that supports under-resourced students seeking degrees at SUNY SCCC by providing tuition assistance.

Brian and I get to choose who will receive the scholarship each year, which then allows us to share Jenson's story with that person while providing a way for them to improve their lives through education. I think Jenson would be proud of the help others are receiving because of him. He always took an interest in those who were not blessed as he was.

About five years after Jenson left this earth I began presenting Bible studies at our county jail, another means of survival for me. Brian has done jail ministry our entire married life, but I hadn't considered it for myself until he needed more women to go into the female floor. This seemed like another opportunity for me to get out of myself and serve others, so I armed myself with my Bible, a devotional, and a CD player and headed into our county jail.

I absolutely love the beautiful women who are incarcerated, whatever the reason they are behind bars. I love their complete honesty about their faith, or lack thereof. I love their really hard questions, their potty mouths, their stories, and the compassion they show me when they learn of Jenson's death. Several are mothers who are separated from their own children, some over and over again, for a very long time, and yet they often shed tears for me upon hearing about my own son's suicide.

When I share about Jenson and how he died, my credibility becomes more tangible to them because I'm no longer just some Jesus-talking woman who has no clue how difficult life really is. My story of pain allows them a safe harbor into which to lower their own damaged and deficient anchors for the hour I'm there.

These women have no false pretensions about how they're to behave. They don't know all the nice religious words we use in church, and they don't care much at all about denominational choices or correct theology. They're broken and hurting like I am, and they have no expectations of what I'm supposed to say or do. They know they're a mess, so their prerequisites for a life of happiness are pretty basic.

Some of the inmates become favorites, and I'm glad they show up multiple times during my once-a-month Saturdays of Bible studies. One woman, whom I'll call Cynthia (not her real name), ended up being one such favorite. She looked like a rather sullen tough cookie the first time she came into the room where we meet but became congenial and engaging after about ten minutes. Playing a song on my CD player is a good beginning for putting the women at ease and loosening tongues when they don't know me. Cynthia liked the song I played that morning, so she mellowed and engaged.

My lesson was about grace. I talk about grace a lot with the women in jail.

Cynthia was asking some really good questions and then shared her experience of attending church when she was younger and struggling to find her way through substantial family dysfunction.

"Years ago when I went to church, I didn't have any money for nice clothes. I wore jeans with holes in them and ratty T-shirts. But you know what, I was there. Nobody seemed to care I was there, though. They cared more about how I was dressed and told me I shouldn't come to church looking the way I did. I couldn't go buy new clothes because I barely had enough money to eat and pay rent," she told us.

I asked her, "How did you feel about all that?"

"I felt like I wasn't good enough to be in church," she responded.

"What did those people's comments make you think about God?" I continued.

Cynthia said, "I for sure didn't think I was good enough for God to care about, either. I was sure He was disappointed in me just the way everyone else was, too, so I stopped going to church."

There was my perfect opening for delving deeper into the grace of Jesus. I asked Cynthia, "What if one of those people who told you to dress better had instead taken the time to get to know you just as you were and made you think you were special even in your ratty jeans and T-shirts? Then, after you knew you were loved by that person, they offered to take you shopping and buy you some new clothes since you couldn't afford any yourself. Yet the whole time they still showed you they loved you and were glad you were in church no matter what you wore. How would you have felt then?"

I went on to explain that's just what Jesus does for us—He loves us just as we are, but doesn't leave us the way He finds us (like Anne Lamott's quote I shared at the end of my first chapter). I told them Jesus cleans us up with His grace and His mercy and clothes us with His goodness. Then, because He loved us first, we love Him.

And as always, every single time I'm there, when I'm speaking to those wonderful women, I realize the lesson is just as much for me as it is for them.

The jail is a safe place for me; sounds like an oxymoron, doesn't it? I get to share my faith and encourage the women with songs, words, and scripture verses, all in the context of their gratefulness for me being there. When I'm with them, my thoughts are not about me as much as they're about bringing a small amount of joy to women who presently don't have much at all. I then get to walk back out into freedom through the gated doors I entered, reminded of what I possess rather than what I've lost.

These tangible means of surviving—resting in beauty, reaching out to others, the scholarship fund, giving gifts of money in Jenson's memory, doing jail ministry—bring encouragement through physical acts of doing something other than sitting at home feeling sorry for myself. There are also unexpected and unanticipated gifts from God, too, flashes of joy I call "GORs"—Glimpses of Redemption that allow survival to reign. GORs are almost mystical in nature and not something for which I spend any time searching. They just seem to appear out of nowhere.

"Glimpse" is an interesting word and can be used as either a noun or a verb. When used as a noun, it's defined as a momentary or partial view. When it's a verb, it means to see or perceive briefly or partially. It's the perfect word for those fleeting moments of deliverance and restoration that bring small twinkles of cheer to a hurting heart.

GORs come in various forms: a song, the written word, an exquisite sunset at the perfect moment, a smile from someone who gets it, and more. They're somewhat holy happenings that remind me there is a hope and a future in spite of how greatly my insides hurt at any particular point. GORs are bestowed at the exact second they're needed; I couldn't live without them.

One of my favorites was a buckled riser during a rehearsal while I sang at Siena College's baccalaureate the May after Jenson died. This buckling happened during an especially difficult song for me to sing because of grief. As the director, my dear friend Kate, watched me slip off the end, she declared Jenson was playing a prank on me to cheer me up. She might have been right; laughter ensued and my smile returned.

Another came when, the year after Jenson died, his best friend ran down the hall at our homeschool co-op and in a manner totally unlike him yelled, "I love you, Mrs. Merriam," after he passed me in the hallway. He learned that from Jenson, and it was Jenson I heard at that moment, a much-needed GOR on a particularly difficult day of missing him.

While I was watching an absolutely gorgeous full moon, it disappointingly disappeared behind a cloud. But it was so big and bright its light continued to glow as it illuminated the cloud in front of it and changed the color from gray to a gorgeous yellowish orange. This GOR came when I needed to be reminded God is still there even when I can't sense His presence.

Another time, when I was feeling especially alone and extremely disquieted, a dragonfly landed on my leg and sat there for a very long time—a GOR reminding me of the beauty of creation and the fact that I'm never alone even if I feel as if I am.

When I was feeling particularly lost and low during our *Seussical* rehearsals the winter after we lost Jenson, one of the cast mothers emailed me out of the blue to find out how I was. She shared with me words from our pastor that were especially meaningful to her at Jenson's memorial service: "Jenson let go of Jesus, but Jesus did not let go of Jenson." I have absolutely no memory of those words spoken that day but so needed to hear them at the precise moment I received the email, a GOR when my heart was particularly painful and my faith was dwindling.

I was going through old magazines and taking off address labels before donating them to the library. There was one, and only one, that had a label with Jenson's name and address on it. It was such an odd thing because none of the magazines were his. It was as if his name was given to me at the precise moment I needed to think about him and remember how much I love him. That label is now a bookmark, a tangible GOR of his official name stamped on paper, declaring he was once a living, breathing person.

These are all gifts of grace from a loving God, balm for my soul, and the assurance that I'm not walking this broken path alone as I hear His whisper-words: "I am He; I am He who will sustain you. I have made you and I will carry you; I will sustain you, and I will rescue you" (Isaiah 46:4). GORs turn my heart back to Jesus and blur my eyes with tears of both sorrow and gratitude at the same time.

Something to Consider: Surviving has been a choice I've made. It hasn't been something someone told me to do, or insisted would be a better use of my time than grieving. We can't force survival on anyone; it has to come from within.

Looking for GORs is something that popped into my head as a message of grace from a loving God. There is always something for which to be thankful, or bring joy, or turn our eyes away from ourselves, but it isn't anyone's job to point that out to us. If we don't sense GORs ourselves, they are of no use to us, because it is the personal noticing of them that offers the redemption.

Allow grace to make GORs evident in someone's grief. It isn't your job to point something out and then tell a grieving person they should appreciate it.

PART THREE

CHAPTER 24

"Tomorrow Shall Be My Dancing Day"
(Endings and Beginnings)

For the last few years of his life, Jenson's final words, upon saying goodbye to family members and close friends, were "I love you. Have fun." It didn't matter if the person was leaving to go to something delightful or something dreaded; Jenson always said the same thing, usually followed by a hug.

This phrase became something of a family joke, and we all started using it when saying goodbye to each other—Brian going to work (not regularly a pleasant thing), me going to an audition (seldom a pleasant thing), the kids going backstage for their recitals, any of us going to see someone we didn't want to see, Tyler going back to college, et cetera. Even as Jenson got in the car with the tester to take his driver's test, I called out, "I love you. Have fun," as all the other parents looked at me skeptically.

One of my treasured gifts, sent to us after Jenson died, is a wooden plaque that always sits in front of his eight-by-ten senior portrait on our dining room table. It was made by a motorcycle friend and reads, "I love you. Have fun." I'm delighted this man wasn't afraid to make that plaque for us. He listened to our Jenson stories at the memorial service and then created something that would speak to our hearts each time we look at it. That is love and, also, greatly appreciated.

I like to know the endings of stories and movies before I read a book or watch a film. Knowing the ending allows me to travel through the action and rest in the storyline more peacefully throughout the suspense and mystery that is the middle of all things—books, movies, and life in general. Because I feel things so deeply, which far too frequently intensifies and heightens my emotions, I enjoy the story journey more if I know whether there is resolution, redemption, or even sadness at the end. Basically, if I know how something ends, I can live through and with the turmoil that lies between the first and last pages of a book, or the first and final scenes of a movie.

My family finds this rather unacceptable; they don't like to know how things turn out beforehand. However, if I harass them enough before I agree to watch or read something, and they already know the ending, they often tell me. I appreciate their generosity in sharing this information against their desires; they do it for me and me alone. Not only am I then more relaxed sitting through the drama, but I probably pester them far less and ask fewer questions, too.

While one day pondering my need to know endings, it occurred to me I already know my own, which allows me greater peacefulness while moving through each day on this crazy planet. I will die, and when I close my eyes in death here, I'll open them in Heaven to see the face of Jesus. I don't know any of the details of how or when I'll die, and I really can't say what Heaven will be like, although I do so hope it looks like the Adirondacks but with shorter winters and no biting bugs.

I do know, however, one day my eternity will stop here so as to continue in Heaven. I look forward to that day. The thought of it doesn't frighten me or cause me unease. I want to be with Jesus, even though I'm certainly and most assuredly neither ready nor desirous to leave Brian, Tyler, or Kalina.

But as much as I want to be with Jesus, I also want to be with Jenson, possibly even more so at this point. I've known Jesus for so much longer than I was allowed to know Jenson here in this life. Plus, Jesus can't fill that Jenson-shaped hole in my heart; He can only cover it with the bandage of His love. But it still oozes Jenson and has left an unhealable wound.

I'm hoping both Jesus and Jenson greet me at the same time when I move to Heaven. I make no apologies for putting them together at my welcome into a glorious eternity. I don't think Jesus has a problem with that, either. Since He's who He is and loves beyond belief, I'm confident He fully comprehends my heart's yearning to see both Him and my son at the exact same moment. What could be better when I leave this earth?! Well, except that my whole family is there, eventually, and we're all together again. That will be perfection!

I do know I'll see Jenson in Heaven. Jesus was his Savior, and Jesus is my Savior, so there you go; Jenson and I will be together for the rest of all time. Then I'll get to be with him longer than I was without him. This knowledge doesn't at all lessen my missing of him here, but it does give me a hope for the future.

Psalm 27:13–14 tells us, "I remain confident of this: I will see the goodness of the Lord in the land of the living. Wait for the Lord; be strong and take heart and wait for the Lord." This earth isn't the "land of the living." It's the land of "sort of holding my breath until I get to Heaven"; the land of "what a mess; I'm glad I don't have to be here forever"; the land of "if this is all there is, whose idea was this"; and more . . . This is only part of our eternity, and in spite of so many beautiful and wonderful things here, the best is yet to come. Jenson is part of that best for me, and although I'm not crossing off calendar days until I get to Heaven, I'm not digging in my heels and shouting, "No, don't take me yet," either.

A few years past I was the singer at a women's retreat where the speaker talked about *kintsugi*, the art of precious scars, an intriguing topic similar to Henri Nouwen's "wounded healer" writings. *Kintsugi* is a Japanese art teaching that broken objects are not something to hide but instead something to display with pride. By repairing broken ceramics, it's possible to give a new lease on life to pottery that, thanks to its "scars," becomes even more refined and beautiful than the original. This traditional art uses a precious metal, often liquid gold, to seam together the pieces of a broken pottery item and at the same time enhance the breaks.

This technique consists of joining fragments and giving them a new, more purified aspect; every piece is unique because of the randomness with which it shatters. Due to the precious metals used in the repaired cracks, *kintsugi* demonstrates that when an object breaks, it can become more valuable. This is the essence of resilience, the regeneration of our brokenness and the beauty it brings to the world around us. Our scars make us more valuable when they are used to give comfort and bring hope to others.

Kintsugi illustrates that brokenness can help shape us into people of even greater desirability and worth. However, as Hospice Chaplain Brent Thomas consoles us, "None of this makes grief easier or diminishes its weight."[43]

We have to decide what we'll do with our grief. Will we honor it or try to hide it? Will we pretend neither we nor anyone else notices it or tell the truth about it? Will we act like nothing about us has been altered or be honest about our scars?

What was previously predictable must change to a new normal so as not to be all-consuming in order to keep up the status quo of who we once might have been. The status quo seems safe, but it's really not, and it most certainly doesn't allow for growth and change.

I choose to see my grief as part of a beautiful story rather than something I need to hide. It's not something to get through, or ignore, or bury. I understand some people are more comfortable with brokenness than others are. I readily admitted my brokenness at the beginning of this book, and I'm neither ashamed of nor apologetic for it. My insides are as messy as the next person's. Some want to hide their brokenness, pretend it doesn't exist, and hope no one sees it behind the covering of their well-placed facade; how deceptive; how sad; how much artistry and grace are missed in the choice of masking.

In *A Wrinkle in Time*, Madeleine L'Engle tells us, "What you think is not the point. What you do is what's going to count."[44] Okay, so what am I going to do, now, ten years down the road from Jenson's suicide? Here's what I've decided, at least at this time; I like to leave the door open for Jesus to move me the way He sees fit. I don't always make right choices when trying to move myself.

I'm going to get up each morning and be grateful for grace. **By Grace I Rise!**

I'm going to love Tyler and Kalina like nobody's business, no matter how they choose to live their lives. Their wounding is equal to my own; their journey is theirs, not mine; and Jesus loves them even more than I do—can that be possible?—so He can work in their lives far better than I can.

I'm going to continue "dancing" with Brian, even when we trip over each other's feet, because we're told in 1 Peter 4:8 to "love each other deeply," and in 1 Corinthians 13:13 "the greatest of these is love." I love my husband.

I'm **NOT** going to say "yes" or "no" simply because other people want me to, but, rather, I'm going to say "yes" or "no" according to what my gut is telling me and trust it's the voice of the Holy Spirit. I'm also going to continue to set boundaries, because Brené Brown tells us some of the most compassionate people are those who have learned to do so.

I'm going to continue to reach out to other mothers who are walking a suicide-survivor road and offer to trek with them. I'm going to do this knowing what Phileena Heuertz says is true: "To the extent we are transformed, the world is transformed."[45] No one should have to sit alone in their pain if they don't choose to do so. People need to see the tangible evidence of promised redemption out of grief in order to continue in hope. And because, as Jerry Sittser states, "sorrow has taken up permanent residence in my heart and enlarged it,"[46] I now have more room to fit others in there too.

I'm going to keep on singing, acting, and speaking so as to hearten and encourage others as well as myself—and also because, selfishly, when I do those things I "feel the pleasure of God," as Eric Liddle said about his running in the movie *Chariots of Fire.*

I'm going to keep my heart and eyes open for new ways to be the hands and feet of Jesus in a world that so markedly needs to see something greater than the ugliness and depravation that regularly show up in the news media and daily living. This world is desperate for something more than what's visible on a TV, computer screen, or cell phone.

I'm going to continue to be honest about my grief and ever-unfolding faith, knowing full well, as a friend posted on Jenson's Facebook, "Grief never ends . . . But it changes. It's a passage, not a place to stay. Grief is not a sign of weakness nor a lack of faith . . . It is the price of love."[47]

I'm going to do the very best I can on this side of Heaven, knowing life on the other side will last for the rest of eternity. I'll try not to let this part pass me by in the hope of getting there sooner, even though I want to see Jenson so very much and find out how he's doing.

I'm going to take what Dawn Miller says to do in *The Journal of Callie Wade* and go for it. She urges us to open our arms to the good moments in our lives and walk outside in the sunshine so its warmth brightens our days. She tells us to not let go of the love around us, no matter what. And she reminds us that, "Sometimes we don't need new scenery, just new eyes."[48]

I pray I have "new eyes" every morning I'm unable to see the grace, mercy, love, and redemption of Jesus. And, only if someone asks, because you know how much I hate unsolicited opinions, I'm going to tell them there's nothing particularly special about me, so if I can survive with the scars of life and death, they can, too.

The musical *Wicked* is one of my favorites. I love the song "For Good" and find myself so often singing it when my thoughts turn to my husband and children and what I've learned from them, especially Jenson since his death. This song's words ring true as to how I view my son and my Savior: "So much of me is made of what I learned from you. You'll be with me like a handprint on my heart."[49] Both Jenson and Jesus have made immense and distinct handprints on my heart. My life and my learning would be far more inconsequential without the imprint of either one of them.

I fell in love with Jesus when I was fifteen, and I fell in love with Jenson more every day from the moment he entered this world. That love didn't end when he died. My love for Jesus hasn't dwindled as my faith has morphed over the years of redefining many things. It's actually grown, as I've learned to let go of things I've been told were imperative but aren't.

"For Good" also contains the line: "I know who I am today because I knew you. Because I knew you, I have been changed

for good."[50] Truly, because I knew Jenson, and because I know
Jesus, I have been changed for good.

Michael Card says, "We're fallen and we're fragile, and
we're not fixable; that's why we have to be redeemed."[51] A suicide death can't be fixed. There's no redefining the way a person dies when they take their own life. The mess of it can't
be cleaned up with nice words or scripture verses. It can't be
redefined with pleasantries or be reinterpreted as less lethal
than it is. The survivors of a loved one's suicide can't be fixed,
either. They live in the perpetual and lifelong damage of their
loved one's agonizing choice.

However, in spite of a decision to end a life, in spite of the
death of one most precious, in spite of the ever-present empty
heart-hole absence of one loved beyond imagining, there is
hope. And it's hope that promises a future Heavenly reunion
with our loved one whose physical body no longer walks in
corporeal companionship with us here on this earth.

It's hope that tells us what we see isn't all there is. Hope
calls to us and proclaims there's redemption that rises out of
pain and sorrow. It pledges regeneration cultivated out of the
compost of our wounded and broken hearts, and it will enlarge
our souls and lives so as to demonstrate our suffering won't
have been in vain.

In his song "Nothing Is Wasted," Jason Gray tells us that
in God's economy of grace, mercy and redemption, beauty will
bloom out of our deepest wounds. This is hope, and its song
sings the lyrics to my own future days on this "swiftly tilting
planet," as Madeleine L'Engle so aptly calls it.

Even though I don't believe the bad things in life come
from the hand of God, I do believe He's the One who redeems
those bad things. We make the messes, and He cleans them
up. He takes our brokenness and turns it into something that
can be used to point us and others to Jesus. He rescues our

hurting hearts and sorrowing souls so as to make us useful as His hands and feet to the people around us.

He's the One who creates beauty out of the ashes of the torched and smoldering ruins of our tragedies. And He does this because of the compassion that flows out of each ventricle of His unfathomably God-sized heart overflowing with endless love. He redeems the messiness and turns it into His own reflection that shines out of all the fractures of our personal brokenness into the splintered and shattered lives of others.

It's because of Jesus, and a substantial amount of arduous and painful work, that I've not been undone by my voyage of grief. I've never been foolish enough to think I could walk this road or do the hard work of healing all by myself. And even though at times I may have felt completely alone, I've traversed this journey with my Savior, who tells me, "And be sure of this: I am with you always, even to the end of the age" (Matthew 28:20).

In other words, even when I can't see Him, or hear Him, or sense His presence, which is more commonplace than I wish I could confess, He's still with me, because He says He is. My hope is in Jesus. He's the one who rescues us and brings redemption out of the tragedies that mar our days and change us forever.

Jenson's empty shoes sit in our vestibule by the front door. I was with him when he bought those shoes eleven years ago. I remember he purchased two pairs that day; we gave the smiling-skull sneakers to his best friend after his death.

At first I left those shoes by the door so Jenson could wear them when he came home again, but he never did come home. Then I left those shoes there because I couldn't bear to part with them any more than I can bear to part with his ashes that claim habitation in our living room. His ashes in residency in our home make him seem somehow closer than if they were buried underground somewhere. His shoes give off the same essence of Jenson's closeness.

Now I keep those shoes there because they're a piece of memory-filled furniture with a history I need to hold on to. Those shoes tell a story of love and of grace and of mercy every time I look at them. They lead me to my story of Jenson, which leads me to my story of Jesus, which leads me to both of their indelible handprints tattooed upon my heart.

Jenson's favorite scripture verse, the one he chose under his senior yearbook picture, is 2 Corinthians 4:18: "So we fix our eyes not on what is seen, but on what is unseen. For what is seen is temporary, but what is unseen is eternal." What we see is not all there is. I desire to be steadfast and brave as I patiently wait for the unseen eternal. But while walking through the visible of the temporary, I want to be a light in a very dark place, like the doctor declared of Jenson when he was ten.

May we live by grace, for it is grace that carries us through all our days, no matter what those days bring as we journey through this present life. May those of us who grieve do it well, so that functional healing comes to us sooner rather than later. And may we go out with these words of the benediction spoken by the pastor at my aunt's memorial service: "May our sorrow not be just a feeling but a calling, so that we may go out and serve as a people who are changed."

Yes indeed, I have been changed for good, and that in itself is something to consider. Not worth the cost of my loss, but changed for good nonetheless. How you define "good" is up to you. Sometimes my own personal definition seems as random as life itself, but I think God is okay with that, and if not, He'll let me know.

So now I close by encouraging you, my readers, to grieve well so you may heal well. Your well-being is worth the fight. Walk into the darkness so you get to the light sooner. Claim and own your survival.

Thank you for taking time to read all I've written. I truly appreciate it. I bid you "goodbye" and end with the words of my wise and wonderful Jenson, the words I heard as I walked out the door on December 23 of 2011: "I love you. Have fun."

And to Jenson, I say, "I'm working on it, I really am. I love you, too."

"A Heart Full of Love"

Shortly after Jenson took his life, some people told me that although I wouldn't get over his death, I would eventually be better, someday. I couldn't fathom the truth of those words at the time, but it has been "someday" for a few years, now, and the reality is, I am better; I really am.

Of course, a different descriptive might be more fitting than "better," since that seems somewhat like a catch-all term for varying opinions of what people mean when they use it. Personally, I think I prefer terms such as: stronger, more useful, more valuable, healthier, more stable, more aware, wiser, more forthright, or more compassionate. These characteristics give greater illumination to my journey of the past ten years. "Better" often refers to recovery from being sick. Grief is a lot of things, but it isn't an illness from which we recover.

As I work on all I need to do for publishing this memoir in a few months, I'm reminded that Christmas of 2021 will be here soon. I wish I loved Christmas the way I used to before 2011, but my reality is, I don't. It's hard to find consistent joy in a season that reminds me more of Jenson's death than of my

Savior's birth. I frequently have to dig down deep and drag the joy up on pulleys of redemption so I'm not a dark blot on the Christmas spirit of the ones I love. No one likes spending time with a dark blot. I want to be winsome and engaging for those precious souls dear to my heart.

Seasonal music is one of the gifts that helps lift me from my loss, so I listen to endless holiday songs and allow them to sing their cheer through my soul on a daily basis. The words and melodies bring a smile to my face. And, as always, the Christmas movies we watched with our whole family when Jenson was alive are still the same ones Brian and I watch every year without him. These movies remind us of his delight in creating his own films, and smiles ensue.

Decorating the house also makes me smile. I remember how much Jenson loved all the Christmas attire of our home, so I continue to decorate for Brian, Tyler, and Kalina, hoping to bring smiles to their faces, too. Our smiles, even if half-hearted, lend comfort and acceptance to our seasonal damage.

We don't do a large tree anymore, though, just something small that sits on a table, and that's okay. Brian and I leave the big trees for Kalina and Tyler to do in the personal living spaces of their adulthood. They each have their individual ornaments now, the ones I collected for them every year until they lived on their own. Jenson's ornament assortment was split between the two of them. Jenson doesn't need them now; he gets to celebrate Christmas with Jesus. Who needs to hang trinkets on a tree when you have Jesus?!

Even though Christmas will never, ever be the same without Jenson here with us, my heart softens a bit each year. The pain of having one of my children missing is not the acute and all-encompassing ache it once was in the preceding years, closer to his death. Continual survival reminds me I will continue to survive; and I do.

I'm no longer angry with God or the people who said and did countless hurtful things in the earlier ensuing years of life without Jenson. Most everyone is broken in some way or another and has their own sadness-collection of life stories that end up being the reasons for the things they say and do. My anger and angst seem to have faded into the setting sun of each day of years gone by as I strive to rest in, and rise by, grace. We all need to give more grace, as well as receive more grace from each other. It really is a must for sane survival.

I want to share the lyrics from "It's Christmas Again," written by my dear sister-in-song Maria Riccio Bryce. She composed this when her own heart was breaking, years before I grew to love her as I do now. The first time I sang this song, tears choked the sound of my voice, and I couldn't finish the melody. Maria's words speak the thoughts and feelings of my heart for the coming Christmas season, as well as every Christmas of the years ahead without Jenson. This song is yet another creation of beauty out of ashes. Maria's ashes mingle with my own, as do all of ours in the reality of personal pain, but healing prevails.

Ev'ry December, as the day fades to sunset,
The earth lies in silence under soft early snow.
The old year is dying; the new one is waiting.
Our hearts whisper gently: "It's Christmas again."

Tho' nothing is certain,
Tho' sadness and sorrow tear open our wounds,
And lay bare all our fears . . .
Still, we watch through the night, for the light of
    the morning
Dawning faithful once more, and: it's Christmas again.

Together, we reach for the hand of forgiveness.
Together, we shelter those lost in the storm.
As the glorious lullaby descends from the heavens,
We hold fast to each other . . . and we remember love.

And now, I end by encouraging you to hold fast to the ones you love the most. Rejoice in a life shared together. Take nothing for granted; you could lose someone in the blink of an eye, forever changing your future days. And by all means possible, be the grace you wish to see in the world.

MUSICAL LISTINGS
BY CHAPTER

"How Could I Ever Know?" from *The Secret Garden*

"Let's Hear It for the Boy" from *Footloose*

"Farewell, Good Angel" from *Jane Eyre*

"Before the Parade Passes By" from *Hello, Dolly!*

"Bewitched, Bothered, and Bewildered" from *Pal Joey*

"What Is This Feeling?" from *Wicked*

"To Life" from *Fiddler on the Roof*

"Get Me to the Church on Time" from *My Fair Lady*

"Dogs in the Yard" from *Fame*

"Moments in the Woods" from *Into the Woods*

"We Make a Beautiful Pair" from *Shenandoah*

"Let Me Entertain You" from *Gypsy*

"Can You Find It in Your Heart?" from *Footloose*

"My Defenses Are Down" from *Annie Get Your Gun*

"The God-Why-Don't-You-Love-Me Blues" from *Follies*

"Don't Fence Me In" from *Adiós Argentina*

"Waitin' for the Light to Shine" from *Big River*

"Shall I Tell You What I Think of You?" from *The King and I*

"Oh, the Thinks You Can Think" from *Seussical: The Musical*

"I Sing the Body Electric" from *Fame*

"They All Laughed" from *Shall We Dance?*

"It Never Entered My Mind" from *Higher and Higher*

"In This Wide, Wide World" from *Gigi*

"Climb Ev'ry Mountain" from *The Sound of Music*

"Tomorrow Shall Be My Dancing Day" (traditional)

"A Heart Full of Love" from *Les Misérables*

QUOTES

1 Madeleine L'Engle, *The Rock That Is Higher: Story as Truth* (New York: Penguin Random House LLC, 2002).

2 Ernest Hemingway/Leonard Cohen.

3 Charles Finney.

4 Charles Dickens, *Dombey and Son* (London: Penguin Books, 2002).

5 Anne Lamott, *Traveling Mercies: Some Thoughts on Faith* (New York: Random House, 1999).

6 Alan B. Hollingsworth, *Flatbellies* (Chelsea: Sleeping Bear Press, 2001).

7 Dawn Miller, *Promiseland: The Journal of Callie McGregor* (Thomas Nelson, 2002).

8 William A. Ritter, *Take the Dimness of My Soul Away: Healing After a Loved One's Suicide* (Harrisburg: Morehouse Publishing, 2004).

9 Jill Kelly, *Prayers for Those Who Grieve* (Irvine: Harvest House Publishers, 2010).

10 William A. Ritter, *Take the Dimness of My Soul Away: Healing After a Loved One's Suicide* (Harrisburg: Morehouse Publishing, 2004).

11 Lysa TerKeurst, *Uninvited: Living Loved When You Feel Less Than, Left Out, and Lonely* (Nashville: Nelson Books, 2016).

12 *Doctor Who*, season 9, episode 11, "Heaven Sent," directed by Rachal Talalay, written by Steven Moffat and Sydney Newman,

featuring Peter Capaldi, Jenna Coleman, and Jami Reid-Quarrell, aired November 28, 2015, on BBC.

13 Jerry Sittser, *A Grace Disguised: How the Soul Grows Through Loss* (Grand Rapids: Zondervan, 1998).

14 Jerry Sittser, *A Grace Disguised: How the Soul Grows Through Loss* (Grand Rapids: Zondervan, 1998).

15 Alan D. Wolfelt, *Understanding Your Suicide Grief* (Fort Collins: Companion Press, 2009).

16 C. S. Lewis, *A Grief Observed* (New York: HarperCollins, 1994).

17 Darrell Scott.

18 Jerry Sittser, *A Grace Disguised: How the Soul Grows Through Loss* (Grand Rapids: Zondervan, 1998).

19 Steve Green, "I Will Go" (Sparrow Records, 2002)

20 William A. Ritter, *Take the Dimness of My Soul Away: Healing After a Loved One's Suicide* (Harrisburg: Morehouse Publishing, 2004).

21 Jerry Sittser, *A Grace Disguised: How the Soul Grows Through Loss* (Grand Rapids: Zondervan, 1998).

22 Kelly Farley and David DiCola, *Grieving Dads: To the Brink and Back* (Aurora: Grieving Dads LLC, 2012).

23 Jerry Sittser, *A Grace Disguised: How the Soul Grows Through Loss* (Grand Rapids: Zondervan, 1998).

24 Erma Bombeck.

25 Nancy Guthrie, *The One-Year Book of Hope* (Tyndale House Publishers, 2005).

26 William A. Ritter, *Take the Dimness of My Soul Away: Healing After a Loved One's Suicide* (Harrisburg: Morehouse Publishing, 2004).

27 Ray Pritchard, *Keep Believing: Finding God in Your Deepest Struggles* (Gideon House Books, 2019).

28 Ray Pritchard, *Keep Believing: Finding God in Your Deepest Struggles* (Gideon House Books, 2019).

29 Jenefer Igarashi, "The Hard Work of Being Job's Wife," Crosswalk.com, September 13, 2011.

30 Carolyn Custis James, *When Life and Beliefs Collide* (Grand Rapids, Zondervan, 2001).

31 Ray Pritchard, *Keep Believing: Finding God in Your Deepest Struggles* (Gideon House Books, 2019).

32 Ray Pritchard, *Keep Believing: Finding God in Your Deepest Struggles* (Gideon House Books, 2019).

33 Kent Annan, *After Shock: Searching for Honest Faith When Your World Is Shaken* (Downers Grove: InterVarsity Press, 2001).

34 Angela Miller, founder of A Bed for My Heart, *You Are the Mother of All Mothers* (Wise Ink Creative Publishing, 2014).

35 William A. Ritter, *Take the Dimness of My Soul Away: Healing After a Loved One's Suicide* (Harrisburg: Morehouse Publishing, 2004).

36 L. B. Cowman, *Streams in the Desert* (Grand Rapids: Zondervan, 1997).

37 Jerry Sittser, *A Grace Disguised: How the Soul Grows Through Loss* (Grand Rapids: Zondervan, 1998).

38 Paulo Coelho.

39 A. Manette Ansay, *Sister* (New York: Avon Books, 1996).

40 Max Lucado, *God Will Use This for Good: Surviving the Mess of Life* (Nashville: Thomas Nelson, 2013).

41 L. B. Cowman, *Streams in the Desert* (Grand Rapids: Zondervan, 1997).

42 William A. Ritter, *Take the Dimness of My Soul Away: Healing After a Loved One's Suicide* (Harrisburg: Morehouse Publishing, 2004).

43 Brent Thomas, hospice chaplain.

44 Madeleine L'Engle, *A Wind in the Door* (New York, Square Fish, 1973).

45 Phileena Heuertz.

46 Jerry Sittser, *A Grace Disguised: How the Soul Grows Through Loss* (Grand Rapids: Zondervan, 1998).

47 Anonymous Facebook post.

48 Dawn Miller, *The Journal of Callie Wade* (New York: Pocket Books, 1996).

49   "For Good," *Wicked*, music and lyrics by Stephen Schwartz, based on the book by Winnie Holzman, 2003.

50   "For Good," *Wicked*, music and lyrics by Stephen Schwartz, based on the book by Winnie Holzman, 2003.

51   Michael Card, *Luke: A World Turned Upside Down* (IVP Books, 2010).

CREDITS

Excerpt from TRAVELING MERCIES: SOME THOUGHTS ON FAITH by Anne Lamott, copyright © 1999 by Anne Lamott. Used by permission of Pantheon Books, an imprint of the Knopf Doubleday Publishing Group, a division of Penguin Random House LLC. All rights reserved.

Excerpts from *Take the Dimness of My Soul Away: Healing After a Loved One's Suicide* by William A. Ritter (Morehouse, 2004) courtesy of the author.

Excerpt from *Prayers for Those Who Grieve* by Jill Kelly (Harvest House, 2010) courtesy of the publisher.

Excerpts from *A Grace Disguised: How the Soul Grows Through Loss* by Jerry L. Sittser (Zondervan, 1998) courtesy of the author.

Excerpt from *Understanding Your Suicide Grief: Ten Essential Touchstones for Finding Hope and Healing Your Heart* by Alan Wolfelt (Companion Press, 2009) courtesy of the author.

Excerpts from *Grieving Dads: To the Brink and Back* by Kelly Farley and David DiCola (Grieving Dads, 2012) courtesy of the authors.

Excerpt from *The One Year Book of Hope* by Nancy Guthrie (Tyndale Momentum, 2005) courtesy of the publisher.

Excerpts from *Keep Believing: God in the Midst of Our Deepest Struggles* by Ray Pritchard (Moody, 1997) courtesy of the author.

Excerpt from "The Hard Work of Being Job's Wife" by Jenefer Igarashi (originally published on Crosswalk.com, Sep. 13, 2011) courtesy of the author.

Excerpt from *When Life and Beliefs Collide* by Carolyn Custis James (Zondervan, 2002) courtesy of the author.

Excerpt from *After Shock: Searching for Honest Faith When Your World Is Shaken* by Kent Annan (IVP Books, 2011) courtesy of the author.

Quote from Angela Miller used with her permission.

"For Good" from the Broadway musical *Wicked*, music and lyrics by Stephen Schwartz, copyright © 2003 Stephen Schwartz. All rights reserved. Used by permission of Grey Dog Music (ASCAP). All rights reserved. Used by permission of Grey Dog Music (ASCAP).

ACKNOWLEDGMENTS

First and foremost, thank you to Jesus, my Savior and Redeemer, for the ability to think thoughts and creatively pen them. I wouldn't be who I am, or where I am, without Him.

Secondly, Brian, Tyler, and Kalina, your love for both Jenson and me allowed me the grace and courage to tell my story throughout these pages. I'm endlessly grateful for you, my heart's delight and "soul cluster" of three. Hopefully, as you read this book, it's obvious how much I love and cherish each of you. Thank you for your unending support, prompting, and generosity in this endeavor, my dear husband. And to my two living, treasured children, I so appreciate you allowing me to use you in this story.

Marion Roach Smith, you took my scattered first draft and gave me pages of notes so I could write a second draft that saved my readers from the deadly boredom of my simply stating events. Where do I begin to tell you how much I learned from your input and knowledge about writing a memoir? My book would not be what it is without your ability to deconstruct my original and tell me how to write a better story so as to draw in my readers and keep them engaged. Thank you for *not* handling me with kid gloves. I'm so grateful I found you.

Mary Sanders Shartle, thank you for reading my second draft and giving me suggestions to make it better, even if I didn't leave out all my hyphenated words! I think they're part of my DNA, so I just couldn't part with every one of them.

And to each of these beautiful women: Kate, Doreen, Betty, Helen, Barb, Lorraine, Mary, and Connie, who believed I had a story to tell and encouraged me to write it out, thank you for cheering me on and spurring me forward to actually follow through to an end product. You were my champions along the way.

Girl Friday Productions was the right choice for my publishing, even if it took me a while to find them or make a decision. If it weren't for Christina, Dave, Bethany, Georgie, and Paul, my amazing team, I'd still be staring at my computer trying to figure out how to get this book into print. Their patience and direction were a perfect fit for me, and I appreciate the expertise they each brought to the table.

JENSON E. MERRIAM SCHOLARSHIP FUND

For those desiring to send a donation to this scholarship fund, you may do so online at: https://sunysccc.awardspring.com /Home/Donor/Merriam

Or you may mail a check to:

SUNY Schenectady Foundation
78 Washington Avenue
Schenectady, NY 12305

Please indicate the Jenson E. Merriam Memorial Scholarship in the memo section of your check.

LIST OF HELPFUL RESOURCES I CONSULTED IN MY GRIEF JOURNEY

American Foundation for Suicide Prevention (AFSP): This is an excellent resource for information regarding suicide. Also, if you are in crisis call (800-273-8255) or text "TALK" to 741741.

Experiencing Grief by H. Norman Wright

Finding Your Way After the Suicide of Someone You Love by David B. Biebel and Suzanne L. Foster

For the Tough Times: Reaching Toward Heaven for Hope by Max Lucado

Good Grief: A Companion for Every Loss by Granger E. Westberg

A Grace Disguised: How the Soul Grows Through Loss by Jerry Sittser

A Grief Observed by C. S. Lewis

Grieving a Suicide: A Loved One's Search for Comfort, Answers, and Hope by Albert Y. Hsu

Grieving Dads: To the Brink and Back by Kelly Farley and David DiCola

Is God to Blame? Moving Beyond Pat Answers to the Problem of Suffering by Gregory A. Boyd

Keep Believing: Finding God in Your Deepest Struggles by Ray
    Pritchard

Lament for a Son by Nicholas Wolterstorff

*Standing in the Shadow: Help and Encouragement for Suicide
    Survivors* by June Cerza Kolf

*Take the Dimness of My Soul Away: Healing After a Loved One's
    Suicide* by William A. Ritter

A Time to Grieve by Kenneth C. Haugk

Understanding Your Suicide Grief by Alan D. Wolfelt

When Mourning Comes by Max Lucado

ABOUT THE AUTHOR

Judi Merriam loves her roles as wife, mother, singer, actor, director, speaker, and writer. When these vocations allow her free time, she can be found hiking, swimming, sewing, reading, or watching British murder mysteries. Her favorite people on earth are her husband, Brian, and her two living children, Tyler and Kalina. Judi makes her home in the historic Mohawk River Valley located between her beloved Adirondack Mountains and New York City. She sings and speaks at various churches and community organizations throughout Upstate New York and has played an extensive number of leading roles, as well as directed, for musical theater companies across the same area. Judi is continuously grateful for the sustaining grace of God as she walks through the messiness of life in this broken world. It is her heart's desire to shine a light of hope into the lives of those who grieve, especially parents who have lost children to suicide.

CPSIA information can be obtained
at www.ICGtesting.com
Printed in the USA
LVHW040801090522
718230LV00025B/241